THE
CHRISTIAN COUNSELOR'S
COMMENTARY

I CORINTHIANS
II CORINTHIANS

JAY E. ADAMS

MID-AMERICA
INSTITUTE FOR NOUTHETIC STUDIES

Institute for Nouthetic Studies, a ministry of Mid-America Baptist
Theological Seminary, 5640 Airline Road, Arlington, TN 38002
mabts.edu / nouthetic.org / INSBookstore.com

I & II Corinthians: The Christian Counselor's Commentary
by Jay E. Adams
Copyright © 2020 by the Institute for Nouthetic Studies,
© 1994 by Jay E. Adams

ISBN: 978-1-949737-23-3 (Paper cover)
ISBN: 978-1-949737-24-0 (eBook)
ISBN: 978-1-949737-29-5 (Hard cover)
Old ISBN: 0-9643556-1-2

Editor: Donn R. Arms

Library of Congress Cataloging-in-Publication Data
Names: Adams, Jay E., 1929-2020
Title: *I & II Corinthians: The Christian Counselor's Commentary*/
Jay E. Adams
Description: Arlington, TN: Institute for Nouthetic Studies, 2020
Identifiers: ISBN (paper) 978-1-949737-23-3 I LCCN: 96178415
Classification: LCC BS2341.2 .A33 I DDC 227.2

Published in the United States of America

To . . .

Bill Goode & Bob Smith

**an incomparable
pair!**

Contents

Preface

"Why a Christian Counselor's Commentary?" Obviously, that is the question some reading the title of this book will ask. It deserves a clear answer. In no way is this commentary, or those on other books of the Old and New Testaments that are planned, intended to replace the many fine standard commentaries already gracing your shelves. Commentaries in this series, rather, are designed to function as a supplement to them. The four gospels, while covering roughly the same territory, each supply additional material that we would all be impoverished to lose. Each is supplemental to the others. As you can see, supplements have an important place to fill.

For too long, in my opinion, the church has suffered in its interpretation and understanding of the Bible from the fact that existing commentaries place an all-too-exclusive emphasis upon grammatical and other critical matters. Please read those words carefully. I am not criticizing the commentators; they have done yeoman work in explicating much of the Word of God. We are all deeply indebted to them. The work done by them is altogether necessary and we have profited immensely from it. My concern, however, is that inadequately equipped to do so, most commentators have had neither the concern nor the practical know-how to bring the Bible to bear upon everyday living as it relates to the problems that Christian counselors face in the process of utilizing the Scriptures in the day-by-day work of ministering the Word. For this reason, in my opinion, many valuable insights have been missed and to that extent the Christian counselor has been impoverished. While I do not pretend to be able to fill in all the gaps, I hope that this endeavor will be appreciated and amplified by others over the years to come, I do think that I have some things to offer that cannot be found elsewhere—enough to make such a work as this of value.

Like the gospel writers, the authors of commentaries have their own individual emphases. That is good. God's Word is larger in scope than any one man or group of men. These emphases do not always contradict one another any more than the distinct emphases of Matthew, Mark, Luke and John. Unlike the gospel writers, however, commentaries do contain contradictions since fallible men wrote them. You may not always agree with my interpretations of passages and, no doubt, will reject some of the applications and conclusions I offer. So be it. I have endeavored, like every responsible commentator on the Bible, to be faithful, but especially so in light of the current penchant for misusing the Bible (sometimes in a near cavalier fashion) to "prove" various counseling positions that the

Bible does not teach. Understand, therefore, that I have taken the utmost care not to stretch passages to say what the Spirit of God never intended them to say. And I have diligently bypassed all uncertain interpretations and applications, no matter how tempting it may have been to include them. I have attempted, rather, to offer solid interpretations upon which you may base your thinking and the directions you take in counseling. To the extent that I have succeeded in reaching these goals, I think you will find this book a genuine aid to counseling.

Much so-called "Christian counseling" is Christian only insofar as the author's Christianity occasionally slips out from beneath the unbelieving counseling orientation of the non-Christian system or systems under which he labors. While decrying this deplorable situation and writing much about what the Bible does have to say about counseling, biblical counselors, until this point, have never systematically gone through the Bible commenting on the various books and passages that appertain to the work of counseling. Nor have they shown how to use them in counseling. This commentary, to my knowledge, is a first. I did something of this sort in a small way through the notes in my *Christian Counselor's New Testament.* And indeed, the translation I made for that publication is virtually the same as the one I am using in this commentary. But for those who believe that, as Paul says, the "man of God" is "adequately supplied for every good task" (II Timothy 3:27) if he understands and properly applies the Bible, a larger, more substantial work of the sort here initiated is needed. I hope that in His providence God will give me the years, the strength and the wisdom to supply it.

This, as I have indicated, is a peculiar sort of commentary. Like some older commentaries that contained notes only on selected portions of the text upon which they thought it particularly important to comment, in these commentaries I shall not address every word and verse, but rather, those from which I am able to deduce teaching and practices that seem especially applicable to the Christian counselor. That is why I call this series of commentaries supplemental. I am attempting to make up for a lack, not to duplicate unnecessarily what already exists.

While that is true, along the way, occasionally I have also remarked on other passages on which I thought I might be able to throw some light, not merely as a sort of bonus, but usually because it was necessary to bring out a translation or interpretation essential to counseling that might otherwise be missed. And, of course, it would not be possible to make observations on passages without indicating something of their essential meanings. Consequently, I have included a running interpretation, sometimes in the form of a paraphrase, that I hope fairly reveals what the writer was saying. I think, therefore, that you will find the commentary of use not only for counseling applications, but also for preaching and for general Bible study. The ministry of the Word, as Acts 20:20 (q.v.) asserts, is twofold. But it is one ministry of one Word in two applications: one public (preaching) and one private (counseling). That these two were intimately connected in the mind of Paul is obvious from his statements not only in that chapter, but also from his remarks in Col. 1:28 and elsewhere. The tragedy in our time is that, unlike the Reformers and vital Christians in every age before, today many separate counseling from preaching, as though they are two distinct activities. They are not. Because they are not, much of what you read here will be useful, I trust, in preparation for messages from the Word of God.

A commentary is a place to comment. Most commentaries comment exclusively about the text. This commentary does that, of course, but largely comments about the *implications of the text* for Christians living, those problems that interfere with it and the solutions to them that Christianity supplies. While much is spelled out in detail, many points are merely suggested: counselors are expected to enlarge on these suggestions as they apply to individual counseling cases.

Explanation

"Why begin with I Corinthians?" you ask. For two reasons. First, as everyone knows, I Corinthians is the epistle of church problems. A large number of problems, ranging from unloving divisions and actions to marriage and sexual difficulties, is addressed in the book. Clearly then, if I were to provide maximum help from the outset, it would seem wise to begin with the book that provides it. Secondly, Paul describes what he is up to in this Book as written "counsel." Listen to his words in I Corinthians 4:14:

> I am not writing these things to shame you, but to counsel
> you as my dear children.

Notice two things about that verse: the word "counsel" that Paul uses is the Greek term *noutheteo* from which I coined the name "Nouthetic Counseling." The word means verbal *confrontation*, out of loving *concern*, designed to *change* another by enabling him from Scripture to think and behave in ways that please God. But secondly, notice that it is a word that has strong familial overtones. Such counseling is clearly pastoral in nature. Paul is not out to shame anyone. He thinks of the Corinthian sinners as his "dear children." He brought them to faith in Christ by preaching the gospel to them and organizing them into a church. And he approaches them in a true filial fashion. People who have latched on to the word "confrontation" in the definition above and ring the changes on it as if it meant beating counselees about the head with rusty chains totally misunderstand biblical counseling. The confrontation is a loving confrontation with the Word of God, calculated to benefit the counselee by bringing him into closer conformity to the will of God. The confrontation must be done for his benefit. Those intentions, so essential to biblical counseling, are clearly present in the verse quoted above. It is fitting then, at the outset of this series of commentaries, to begin with I Corinthians since it not only provides so much help for the biblical counselor but also because it sets the proper tone and atmosphere for all those that follow.

Before I proceed further, I wish to thank Ms. Cheri Burress for typing the manuscript.

Introduction to
I Corinthians

What you will now read is not a detailed introduction to I Corinthians. That may be found in most commentaries and New Testament introductions. Rather, in the paragraphs that follow, I plan to touch briefly on several points that, because of their pertinence to the commentary and to an understanding of the basic situation that Paul faced when writing, seem important to include.

Consider the book as a whole. Often counselors are perplexed at the outset of a counseling case by the sheer magnitude of particulars in the situation. Frequently, they give up or fail because they do not know how to begin. They defeat themselves because they try to handle mingled data. They do not realize that it is the complexity of the case that makes it appear so formidable. When they allow the various elements of the case to remain mixed together, counseling tends to become mixed up too. In listening to reports about the church at Corinth, doubtless Paul too may have been confused at first. So many things were wrong. Probably, as the reports arrived, the data (as they usually are) were presented in a conglomerate form. After all, the problems involved the same basic group of people, closely tied together in so many interrelated ways. It would be unusual if, at the outset, the situation at Corinth did not seem formidable, even to Paul.

So, how did he handle that difficulty? *He sorted things out.* Good counselor that he was, one by one, he took up each matter separately until he had exhausted the lot: pride, division, false wisdom, sophistry, challenge of his apostolic calling, incest, lawsuits, delinquency in fund raising, divorce and other marriage problems, abuse of gifts, lack of love, disorder in meetings, denial of the bodily resurrection, etc. By sorting them out, he removed the principal difficulty that the counselor meets when he first begins to thread his way through a counselee's presentation: complexity. Paul *simplified* things for himself and his counselees. *That* was a large step toward dealing with the problems themselves.

Sometimes, merely sorting problems out for the counselee itself is a key to their "ultimate solution." You can tell when this is happening because as you lay things out in order, taking them up one at a time, he often sighs in relief, comes alive and frequently begins to make suggestions about what might be done to resolve the issues. Bringing order out of chaos is God's way of acting, as the first couple of verses of Genesis (as well as comments about order in I Corinthians that we shall examine later) indicate. In counseling, clearly it is one important means of generating hope for the counselee (and the counselor!). Sorting things out so that they can be dealt with separately demonstrates that the seemingly out-of-hand and unmanageable is already beginning to be handled and managed—though, of course, only in a preliminary way. Naturally, this hope will quickly vanish if it is not followed by further progress. But early hope is a significant factor in setting the scene for future progress.

"Well, I can see that, but where do I begin?" you may ask after listening to the complicated, contradictory, tangled picture painted, say, by counselees Frank and Fran. "It's all so confusing; how can it ever be unraveled?" By the imagery you used, you have actually put your finger on the answer to your question—you can unravel the mess *by unraveling it!* Look for the separate threads that hang out: mother-in-law problem (hers, of course), work, sexual difficulties, poor communication—grab one. Keep pulling on that thread until you come to an end. You will have isolated, sorted out, unraveled one strand. Then deal with it biblically. Grab another and pull it loose, then another and another until the whole comes apart like a sweater pulled to pieces. Sort out the reds, the greens, the whites, and lay them side-by-side in orderly fashion—just as Paul did. The key to doing this is to take one thread at a time and continue to pull on it until it comes untangled and lies alone. Then, and then only, can its length be determined with any sort of accuracy. While it is still part of a whole, adding to the complexity of the case, it might have seemed endless. Moreover, while it was still intertwined with the rest, it could not be appraised properly, and the whole seemed larger than it now does with the thread extracted. But now, there it lies, manageable, less formidable, unraveled.

It is possible, of course, that when dealing with one problem, you may discover that another may be so tightly tied to it that at least some aspect of the second problem must be dealt with in order to complete what you are doing about the first. In such cases, don't allow yourself to become sidetracked. Deal with the second problem *only insofar as it bears upon the first.* If, for instance, in counseling Fran and Frank about sex, you discover that the mother-in-law problem is what is getting in the way of proper sexual relations because of words and attitudes that have developed out of it, you may have to do one of two things: either stop and solve the mother-in-law problem in part (but only do so if it is basic to solving the other), or more likely, help the involved parties seek forgiveness all around for everything that has gone wrong in their relationships with a promise to seek God's answer to what led to that difficulty when the discussion of the matter at hand has been completed. Be sure not to lay down a green thread, not fully dealt with, in order to pick up a red one, unless it is absolutely necessary to handle the red thread to solve problems connected to the green one. Counselees are notorious for their tendency to roam from one problem to another before completing any. Don't allow them to do so. You must maintain full control over the counseling session, focusing the discussion at all times upon the one problem you are considering, as Paul did. Just go through the book of I Corinthians and notice how Paul does it. He never loses track of where he is going; rather, relentlessly he takes up one problem after another, considering each, until he is finished.

The analogy to the unraveled sweater does not hold in all respects you can see, because what sometimes appears to be a whole made up of separate parts may, in fact, be two or more wholes, each consisting of several parts. This kind of confusion often occurs when the counselee has had a problem for quite some time, and though new complicating problems have been added to it, he still thinks of his problem in its original form, as if no additions or changes had occurred. Usually, complicating problems occasioned by new events, faulty attempts to solve the original problem (putting six knots in the fishing line while trying to untie one), and erroneous interpretations of the situation must be handled first. Often you cannot get to the original except by untying the other six.

A common example of a complicating problem that must be solved first is the deterioration of relationships between persons who have been unable to solve some original problem. Bitterness, resentment, aloofness, or whatever form this deterioration may take has grown so strong that it colors everything. A good example in I Corinthians is the problem of lawsuits that Paul handles in chapter six. Significantly, notice that he doesn't even tell us what the issues were that occasioned the suits. Obviously, lawsuits had so complicated the relationships of those involved that there was no sense trying to consider the offenses involved until the more basic matter of Christians taking one another to law was settled. That complicating problem was so large that it stood in the way of doing anything constructive about the differences that occasioned the lawsuits. Solutions to the original issues, even plainly and convincingly presented from the Scriptures, would likely do no good until the bad relations stemming from the Scriptures and the serious error, evidenced in taking one another to court, had been dealt with. Until repentance, forgiveness, willingness to drop the suits and reconciliation are effected, persons involved will raise objections, find fault and cast doubt upon any solution to the original problems.

3

A novice counselor may look on those responses as simple disobedience and disbelief. Disobedience and unbelief? Surely. But *simple*? No. Matters are complex; complicated by sinful attitudes of the counselees toward one another. So, until the counselor separates the relational problem from the issues, he will get nowhere. *Issues are resolved by Christians in the right relationship to God and their brothers.* At any rate, that seems to be how Paul viewed difficulties at Corinth. Beneath all other problems lay a lack of love for one another and God. He seemed to think it necessary to discourse on this important fact, you remember, in a long, invaluable chapter. This excursus he placed squarely in the center of his discussion of the unloving use of gifts in Corinthian worship. Presumably he thought it not enough to show them the proper way to use gifts but was concerned about the greater problem of bad attitudes in doing so. The former could not be satisfactorily resolved apart from resolving the latter.

So, sorting out problems, asking "How many are there?", "Of what sorts are they?", separating original problems from complicating ones and distinguishing issues from relationships, is, as Paul seemed to understand, important in helping counselees. This we can learn from considering the letter of I Corinthians as a whole.

While Paul makes it clear that what he is writing is "counsel," (he uses the word *noutheteo,* remember) there is every indication that writing is not the best form of counseling. Other apostles also considered writing inadequate for the purpose (cf. II Jn. 11; III Jn. 13,14). Paul was anxious to visit the Corinthians (see Ch. 16); you can imagine how much better it would have been to deal with problems in person. This may be seen particularly in his second letter (which we shall consider at the proper place). It is hard to know how the one with whom you are communicating will respond to your words when you are not present to receive immediate feedback. Yet, for judicious reasons, Paul refrained from satisfying his curiosity about the church at Corinth, passed by the city and instead, wrote them this letter which, in God's providence, has been such a blessing to all of God's churches ever since. Counselors should, as one consideration then, remember the power of writing as one form of counseling—something that I have inadequately stressed in my books prior to this time. Yet remember that counseling by mail, at best, is but a pale substitute for counseling in person.

Now, just a word before we look at the book of I Corinthians chapter by chapter. As we move through the book, I shall focus on two major factors: *what* Paul does and *how* he does it. While it is true that his main emphasis is on the content, not on the manner in which that content is conveyed, nonetheless Paul's deep concern to present what he has to say in ways that will commend themselves to his readers crops up at many points. He is not afraid of the offense of the cross; he *is* concerned about the offense of the preacher of the cross. Therefore, we shall make both a matter of study as we proceed (after all, both are the product, not only of Paul, but also of the Holy Spirit). I do not intend, however, to say such things as "now we are dealing with content; now we are dealing with Paul's manner of presenting it." So, as you read, you may want to take a couple of sheets of paper, labeling the first "Principles" and the second "Practices" and make a running list of each for yourself. You will find Paul's letter rich in both.

We are now prepared to consider the book by chapters.

CHAPTER 1

1 Paul, called to be an apostle of Jesus Christ by God's will, and our brother Sosthenes,

2 to God's church in Corinth, to those who are sanctified by Christ Jesus, and called saints together with all those who in every place call upon the Name of our Lord Jesus Christ, Who is their Lord and ours.

In this chapter Paul strongly emphasizes background. He explains how he knew what he knew, from whom he had obtained such information and, basically, how he intended to deal with it. This emphasis was important because it established the fact that he was not working with slander or gossip or third hand material but that respected persons in the Corinthian Church itself, whom he names, were his first hand source of information. Counselors, take heed!

Counselors who accept "privileged" information (where someone says, "Now, I think you should know about this, but don't tell anyone that I told you") wrong all parties involved. The counselor is over a barrel: he can't divulge information lest he be asked for his sources, or he does and refuses to name the accuser. If he does the latter, he becomes a talebearer (Proverbs 11:13; 20:19), otherwise known as a gossip. Either way he is wrong and sins. The counselee is in difficulty: he doesn't know that others know, or confronted with data, he cannot question his unknown accuser or evaluate the source. And the informer is allowed to indulge in the sins of gossip or slander. Doubtless Paul received the data about affairs at Corinth upon condition that he could name his sources. And he did so (v. 11). Counselors must be careful about such matters; it is the tendency of many (perhaps most) counselees to offer privileged information. Be alert, or before you know what has happened, you will find yourself accepting it. In Christian counseling, there is no place for a conspiracy of silence.

Note also that it was *more than one* member of Chloe's household (Chloe, by the way, means "the blonde") upon which Paul's data rested. He should have been careful to establish every fact by two or more witnesses (cf. II Corinthians 13:1). Counselors must be every bit as careful in handling and presenting charges.

It is interesting that at the outset (v. 2), in a double-barreled way, Paul calls the Corinthian Christians "saints" and reminds them that they have

7

3 May help and peace from God our Father and from the Lord Jesus Christ be yours.

4 I thank God always about you for God's grace that has been given to you in Christ Jesus

---

been "sanctified in [or 'by'] Christ Jesus." Moreover, he identifies them with other Christians everywhere: "...who in every place call upon the Name of our Lord Jesus Christ." As this letter unfolds, one becomes more and more convinced that the Church at Corinth had as many—or more—problems as any other Church to which Paul wrote in the New Testament corpus of his letters. Because he must correct so many ways and reprimand them so severely, they might misunderstand, thinking that he was about to abandon them. How many counselors today would give up on people like these in Corinth? Probably more than would continue to work with them. Paul never lost hope. If the power of God saved them, so too could the Spirit continue to change and sanctify them. Let Paul's faithful persistence encourage you when dealing with difficult cases.

Paul wants to assure them that he does not think more highly of other congregations than he does of them. He is concerned, right away, to assert the fact that they have all the requisite resources for overcoming those problems that any other church has (1:5). He will not allow them to think of themselves as "less spiritual" and, therefore, less able to change. Problems they may have—galore—but Jesus Christ, who made them "saints" (lit., "set aside ones") and sanctified them (lit., "set them aside") is able to effect the changes needed to glorify His Father in the heavens. He will not write them off—as many of us might have done. But he takes the time to patiently work with them, dealing with problem after problem. Indeed, he even "thanks God" for them (v. 4).

The patience of an expert counselor is seen throughout I Corinthians in the loving, caring, long-suffering attitude that pervades the epistle. The Corinthians, though disobedient, are still God's children. The tendency among many counselors is to move along to a more promising case if the one at hand proves difficult and disappointing. Not so the apostle. And as we shall see when we come to the second epistle to the Corinthian Church, Paul's loving patience paid off!

Paul is going to have to say some hard things in the course of his letter. He will call for many radical changes. How can the Corinthians expect to make them? They seem so weak, so unable to understand and obey. Up front, Paul tells them of the mighty power that is available. Grace (here,

5   since you were enriched by Him in everything, in every word and all knowledge,
6   even as the testimony about Christ was confirmed among you,
7   with the result that you don't lack any gift as you are waiting for the revelation of our Lord Jesus Christ.

---

the word means "help") and peace (that sense of well-being that comes from pleasing God) from their Father and from the Lord Jesus are attainable (v. 3). Plainly, by these words, Paul identifies them as children of God and encourages them. He continues to strengthen their resolve by mentioning the many gifts granted them, as well as the God-given supply of truth and knowledge (much of which came in extraordinary ways) that were theirs (vv. 4, 5). Indeed, Paul says that they had been given *everything* (v. 5). The supernatural gifts that they received "confirmed" that they were true children of God and that the Spirit was at work among them to provide all they needed (v. 6).

How important it is, as soon as possible, for counselors to point counselees to the resources available for bringing about change. Counselors should become aware not only of the significance of doing so, but also of how to do it. Unless what these are is spelled out with some clarity (today, you will no longer refer to the extraordinary gifts, of course, but to God's Word in completed written form), the counselee may listen to guidance and exhortation only halfheartedly with a "Well, maybe Paul can do it, but I'm not Paul" attitude. By affirming that they didn't lack any gift (v. 7), Paul with one stroke of the pen generated hope and removed all possible excuses. While it cannot always be the first thing out of a counselor's mouth, surely up front somewhere, he must give similar assurance.

Paul is going to confront much sin and error in this church. And as you have seen, in Christ's Name he will demand change. Paul certainly is not a counselor who "accepts" the Corinthians as they are. He does not deal with this congregation nonjudgmentally. He goes after every problem, like a cat pouncing on a mouse. Nor does he think it too much to handle many problems in one letter. The conventional counseling "wisdom" of our time is thrashed by Paul's very directive methods, methods denigrated even by many Christians who counsel. Yet, in it all don't miss the fact that Paul is not problem-centered. His orientation is to honor His God by helping bring about those solutions that God, through the Spirit's inspiration, gave him. Because he believes in the powerful grace of God, he is solution-oriented to the hilt.

8   He will also confirm you to the end, so that you won't be called to account by anyone on the Day of our Lord Jesus Christ.
9   God, Who called you into fellowship with His Son Jesus Christ our Lord, is faithful.

It is instructive also to note that Paul directs his counselees to God, not to themselves, himself, or any counseling system or techniques as the source of help (vv. 3-7). That is rare in so-called "Christian counseling" today. Yet if somewhere near the outset there is no Pauline-like direction, a counselee has the right to question whether what purports to be biblical is really so. In Corinth, as in most serious counseling, there is much to be accomplished and many difficult changes to be made. Sometimes people doubt the possibility of such radical change, but when reading words like those in verses 3-7, all doubt about whether the changes could be made should evaporate. If God requires them, and if He provides the ways and means, then, no doubt, all He requires can be attained. The responsibility for failure should there be such, is rightly placed where it ought to be placed—not on Paul, nor on God, but squarely on the counselee. And the assurance Paul gives is based on God's faithfulness to those in fellowship with His Son (v. 9).

And, as if that were not enough, Paul offers great encouragement when he says that God will not give up on them, but will continue to work in them to the end—until the day of Christ. And he affirms that *He will change them* so that they would not be called to account on that Day (v. 8). What a boost to the morale of a congregation that must have known it was in serious trouble! And what an encouragement to the apostle Paul who knew that what he was writing was true—by God's marvelous grace, even the *Corinthian* church could be presented to the Lord Jesus as a chaste bride without spot or wrinkle or any such thing! When counseling difficult people you should take heart from these words. When you feel like giving up, say to yourself, "But Paul didn't give up on the Corinthians," and then reread this passage anew. Counselor, until you have such hope in you heart for your counselee—no matter how feeble his Christian life—you are not ready to counsel. He already has enough doubt and uncertainty of his own; he doesn't need your less-than-hopeful attitude added to it. Read the Scriptures yourself, believingly, until out of them the Spirit of God generates the hope and expectation you need to communicate the same to your counselee.

10 Now I urge all of you brothers, by the Name of our Lord Jesus, to agree about what you say, so that there won't be any divisions among you, but that you will be bound together by the same attitudes and opinions.

11 I say this, my brothers, because I have been told by some members of Chloe's household that there are disputes among you.

12 What I mean is that each of you is saying things like this: "I am of Paul," or "I am of Apollos," or "I am of Cephas" or "I am of Christ."

13 Has Christ been divided? Paul wasn't crucified for you, was he? And you weren't baptized into the name of Paul, were you?

14 I am thankful that I didn't baptize any of you except Crispus and Gaius,

15 so that no one can say that you were baptized into my name.

16 (Oh yes, I did baptize the household of Stephanas too; beyond that I don't remember baptizing anyone else.)

In verses 10ff., Paul takes up the problem of disunity in the Corinthian church. He expects divisions among them to be "mended" (the word in verse 10 was used of mending torn fishing nets). He pictured the Corinthian Church as a ripped seine that needed mending before it could function as it was intended. Attitudes and opinions differed widely about many things (v. 10), but largely these differences stemmed from setting men on pedestals. These in turn were played off over against one another (v. 12). Note particularly, it was not only those who set up apostles and teachers as their guides but those who, in a pious vein, even dared to set up "Christ" against His own apostles ("we are of Christ") that Paul confronts! Paul is aware of their super-pious claim and demolishes it. Watch out for the (not truly) "pious" counselee who always has a "spiritual" word of explanation why he is right and all others are wrong. Paul does not hesitate to include him in the list with other divisive persons. It is not the name that one uses or the pious language he employs that counts; the issue is whether or not he is dividing the church of Christ.

While he is arguing against divisions, an interesting fact emerges: Paul goes to extra lengths to state himself accurately, lest anyone jump on what he has to say and, by noting some insignificant error of fact, divert the discussion away from the crucial issue. Counselees do this all the time; some are past masters at it. Do as Paul did: if you misstate yourself or do not state your point quite clearly, go back over what you said and be more precise (note vv. 14-16). Paul was not about to provide a handle for any who might want to grab it. It is important for a variety of reasons to qualify and define carefully. Probably people were pouncing on words

17 Christ didn't send me to baptize, but to announce the good news; not with clever words, lest the cross be emptied of its significance.

18 The message of the cross is foolishness to those who are perishing, but to us who are being saved it is God's power.

19 It is written: **I shall destroy the wisdom of the wise and I shall set aside the intelligence of the intelligent**.

20 Where is the wise man? Where is the scribe? Where is the modern debater? Hasn't God made the world's wisdom foolish?

21 Since in God's wisdom the world didn't know God by its wisdom, God was pleased to save those who believe through the foolishness that we preach!

22 While Jews ask for signs and Greeks seek for wisdom

23 we, on the contrary, preach about a crucified Christ; a stumbling block to the Jews and foolishness to the Greeks.

---

and various other minutiae. Accuracy, exactness, further qualification and restatement are all crucial in counseling—but especially when you are dealing with hairsplitters. Paul's care about such matters alerts us to how important he thought the manner in which he dealt with matters is.

Incidentally, notice that Paul distinguished between baptism and preaching the gospel. Churches that identify the two obviously err in doing so. You will occasionally meet such persons, or those influenced by them, in counseling. It is good, therefore, to keep this critical word by Paul in mind for use on such occasions. Clearly Paul did not consider baptism as an element of the gospel as they do.

In verses 18-31, Paul takes time to contrast the world's wisdom and persons wise in worldly ways with God's wisdom and the kind of persons that God ordinarily chooses ("not many noble...wise," etc.) And at the conclusion of the chapter he makes it clear to the Corinthians that all they have—wisdom, righteousness, sanctification or redemption—is theirs, not by their own wisdom or worth, but purely in Christ. Therefore he insists that they should stop their unholy, divisive boasting and unitedly "boast in the Lord!" as he reminds them the Scriptures say they should (vv. 30, 31).

In the course of this discussion, Paul distinguishes the particular difficulties of both Jews and Greeks (v. 22). All who simplistically see only one basic problem behind all the seemingly different difficulties presented by counselees (as some so-called "Christian" counseling theorists contend) should notice how Paul distinguishes different obstacles that people with distinct cultural and religious backgrounds must overcome. Not everyone's problems are the same. Canned approaches, used with every

24 But to those who are called, both to Jews and to Greeks, Christ is God's power and God's wisdom.

25 God's foolishness is wiser than human wisdom, and God's weakness is stronger than human strength.

26 Just take a look at your call, brothers: not many were wise persons (by human standards), not many were powerful, not many were of nobility.

27 But God chose what the world considers foolish things to put wise men to shame. God chose what the world considers weak things to put strong things to shame.

28 And God chose what the world considers unworthy and what it treats with contempt and even the things that it considers to be nothing to make useless those things that are supposed to be something

29 so that nobody might boast in God's presence.

---

counselee heedless of differences, will lead to failure most of the time. Good counselors know from the start that there are fundamental problems that people in certain situations are likely to manifest. That is why Paul could characterize Jews and Greeks as he did. But that took some thought on his part beforehand. One does not usually come up with such ideas on the spot. They are the product of research, observation and thought. In his discussion he has boiled all down to the irreducible minimum: the core problems are identified. Every counselor, in each case, ought to be able to do the same.

In verses 19-21, Paul shows the foolishness of Christians who rest on worldly wisdom. This foolishness is seen especially in counseling where there is no consensus; nothing but proliferation. Counselors, moving from fad to fad, show thereby the futility of worldly systems and demonstrate how God is already destroying the "wisdom of the wise," as each new view cancels out the previous one. He loves to show how, in His time and way, He can "set aside" intellectuals (v. 19), who contradict His Word. In His providence, God does this even by using their own kind to bring it about. God is determined to "shame" those who treat His Word with contempt (vv. 27, 28). And He intends to do so—in every area—by calling into His church those who are "weak," those "not noble" and those who are "nothing," fitting them to outshine the self-styled intellectuals of this world by the application of Christian truth to life. Perhaps this divine dynamic is seen as plainly as anywhere in the field of counseling.

In contrast to the dividers, throughout this section Paul points to unity in Christ. He is not only the great Divider (between believers and

30 By Him you are something in Christ Jesus, Who became our wisdom, that is, our righteousness, sanctification and redemption from God
31 so that what is written might be obeyed: **Let the one who boasts, boast in the Lord.**

---

unbelievers), but He is also the great Unifier (of God's children). He is the One Who, properly understood and humbly served, erases all the artificial, harmful lines that Christians draw between themselves. When helping divided people in counseling (one of the principal tasks of every counselor), you will proceed properly only when you bring them together through the life and work of Jesus Christ. Pragmatic goals or emotional appeals do not unite in lasting or proper ways. All issues and relationships that need attention must be handled in the light of Christ's commands and His declared sufficiency (Matthew 28:18-20). And incidentally, verse 29 is a powerful rebuke to proud persons bent on having their own ways despite the fact that by their pride they scandalously divide Christ's church.

All in all, chapter one sets out major themes that should undergird all that Paul will say in subsequent chapters. It is well, therefore, to understand the full import of his words so as to profit in the early sessions of counseling with your counselees. Take time to study this chapter of I Corinthians in depth, and return to it frequently for encouragement, guidance and help.

CHAPTER 2

1 When I came to you brothers, I didn't come announcing the revealed secret of God in high-flown speech or wisdom,
2 because I determined to know nothing while I was among you except Jesus Christ and Him crucified.
3 I was with you in weakness and in fear and with much trembling.
4 I didn't deliver my message or preach in persuasive words of wisdom, but with proof and power provided by the Spirit,
5 so that you might not place your faith in human wisdom, but rather in God's power.

The discussion in the second chapter grows out of the latter part of the first but forms a unit of its own. The intention of this chapter is to expand thoughts previously expressed about the wisdom of the world and the wisdom of God by disclosing how they effect those who depend upon each. The contrast between the two set up in Chapter One is continued but more in terms that demonstrate why persons involved make the choices they do. In essence, Paul declares "unless you have been regenerated by the Spirit of God, you will not, indeed *cannot*, accept the wisdom that comes from God." Looking at this chapter as a whole, we shall deduce some principles that are extremely important to all counselors. Unless these are understood and their implications are worked out in one's counseling, it will remain subchristian and unfruitful.

Paul opens the present discussion with an account of his own personal experience among the Corinthians. He wants them to remember how it came about that they were saved. It was not through the power of elocution or his intellectual prowess that this occurred, but through the simple, clear, unadorned preaching of the gospel (vv. 1, 2). As a matter of fact, says Paul, I was deeply concerned (that's the meaning of his commonly-used expression, "weakness, fear and much trembling") for your conversion to be a real work of the Spirit and not some bogus repentance that grew out of a purely emotional or intellectual experience generated by sophistic tricks of the trade (vv. 4, 5). He refrained from using any persuasive arguments that did not grow out of the biblical teaching about the death and resurrection of Jesus Christ (v. 2). All proof and power had to come from God's Spirit alone (v. 4). Much could be said about some of

6 Of course we do speak wisdom among those who are mature, but it isn't modern wisdom or a wisdom that comes from modern day leaders, who are coming to nothing.

7 Rather, we speak about God's secret wisdom that has been hidden, that God predestined before time began for our glory.

8 No modern day leaders have known this; if they had known they wouldn't have crucified the Lord of glory.

9 But as it is written:

---

the televangelists and the revivalists who work up emotions to secure decisions, while failing to present the gospel itself, so that "converts" have little or no understanding of what it is that they are converted from or to. Down the road, counselors meet up with these people who were never saved at all but had only some emotional "experience." But I will not labor this point.

One thing I do want to mention in regard to the issue is this: because many people are emotionally oriented when they come for counseling, it is easy to convince them that they can receive help by appealing to those emotions. Following Paul's clear example and adopting his concern, counselors themselves, must take great care not to deceive people into pseudo-experiences that only simulate the genuine, internal work of the Spirit. To always avoid this is an absolute dictum for every biblical counselor. Whenever doubtful, the counselor should openly warn the counselee that any commitment or decision made must be made to please Christ, not in order to satisfy some emotional drive, or to obtain some desired end.

Having written this introductory word, which appeals to their own knowledge of what the Holy Spirit did for them through the simple preaching of the gospel message, Paul now proceeds to show why it is that some do, and others don't, welcome the Spirit and the wisdom of God. It is not that we have nothing wise to offer, nor that he is opposed to wisdom, Paul assures them, but his wisdom is different from that which the world offers: it is the eternal wisdom of God that now has been made known by God's Spirit (vv. 6, 7). That wisdom today, as you know, is found in the Scriptures. Such wisdom, he explains, is unknown to the modern-day leaders of the world—the philosophers and teachers whose thought dominated the Greek-speaking community spread around the Mediterranean are those he had in mind. This is evident from the fact that, had they known it, the world-rulers who adopt such thinking would never have slain the glorious Savior of the world (v. 8).

What the eye hasn't seen and the ear hasn't heard, and what hasn't been conceived by the human heart, is what God has prepared for those who love Him.

10 To us God revealed it by His Spirit. The Spirit searches into everything, even the deep thoughts of God.

11 Who knows the thoughts of a person except the spirit of the person in him; so too no one knows God's thoughts except God's Spirit.

12 Now we haven't received the world's spirit but the Spirit Who is from God, so that we may know that which God has freely given to us.

13 It is these things about which we speak, not in words taught by human wisdom but in those that are taught by the Spirit, combining spiritual teaching with spiritual words.

We are beginning to see that just as there are two types of wisdom, so also there are two types of people: those who espouse one and those who accept the other. Paul's point is that those who reject the gospel have no capacity to do otherwise. In the room where you sit, there are sights and sounds that you do not see or hear because you are incapable of doing so. But if you turn on a TV set you could see and hear both. "Natural" persons—people to whom nothing supernatural has ever happened—are persons who possess no capability to pick up spiritual truth and influences. As Paul put it, "What eye hasn't seen and the ear hasn't heard, and what hasn't been conceived by the human heart, is what God has prepared for those who love Him" (v. 9). Paul's point is that the unregenerate person cannot receive the things of the Spirit of God, because they are spiritually understood (which is to say, unless the Spirit works a work of regeneration to enlighten them, they are incapable). It is as though the Holy Spirit dwelling within the believer is the receiving set that others lack.

God's truth is welcomed by those whom the Spirit enlightens. By His holy working in their lives, they are made capable of understanding what others cannot—"even the deep thoughts of God" that He has searched out and revealed (vv. 10, 11). Otherwise it is impossible to know God's thoughts. It was the Holy Spirit's task to supervise the writing of the Scriptures. Those Scriptures are a record of the thoughts of God, applied to life situations, that the Spirit, through chosen men, has made known to those whom He has enabled to love God (cf. Romans 5:5). By that self-same Spirit, Who illumines God's children, they are able to know all those things that God has "freely given to us" (v. 12b). But those who have never been born again—natural (lit., "soulish") persons—neither welcome His biblical teachings nor are able to understand them (v. 14).

14 But a natural person doesn't welcome the teachings of God's Spirit; they are foolishness to him, and he isn't able to know about them because they must be investigated spiritually.

15 But the spiritual person is able to investigate everything while (on the other hand) nobody has the ability to investigate him.

16 **Who has known the Lord's mind; who will instruct Him?** But we have the mind of Christ.

Instead, they scoff at, or turn their backs on them, calling them foolish (v. 14). The only way in which the Spirit's Word may be successfully investigated is "spiritually"—that is, by the ability He, Himself, imparts to all Christians to do so. "Those," as Paul tells us elsewhere, "who are in the flesh [a term similar to "soulish," meaning an unbeliever] cannot please God" (Romans 8:8). In contrast, the believer in Christ, because of the presence and work of the Holy Spirit Who is at work within him, can successfully investigate and understand "everything" (v. 15). That is to say, he has the capacity to receive and properly interpret God's revealed truth. As a result, it is possible to say that potentially he has "the mind of Christ" (v. 16). He is capable of thinking God's thoughts after Him. The unbeliever, all the time, hasn't got a clue. And in that fact lies an important difference.

It is just this difference between the regenerate and the unregenerate person that makes *all* the difference in counseling. As in education, the wise Christian teacher recognizes that not all are equally educable, so too in counseling you must distinguish between those who can understand and effectually apply the Word of God to their lives in order to make those changes that please God and those who cannot.

Few facts could be more important to the Christian counselor than those that are taught in this chapter. They are foundational to all effective counseling. The counselor must recognize that all counseling that purports to be Christian *must* bring about change *that is pleasing to God*. But if unregenerate persons can neither understand nor do those things that God requires, it is impossible to counsel them. The important truth for counselors, therefore, is that they *should not attempt to counsel unbelievers*. Since counseling is the instruction and application of truth that enables one to love God and his neighbor (as Jesus summed up the content of Scripture), counselors must reckon with the fact that the love of God (love He both gives and accepts) is not "poured into our hearts" until the Spirit of God is (Romans 5:5). There is no way that a "natural" person,

18

(who is "in the flesh," not in the Spirit) can make changes that please God. Such changes are part of the sanctifying work of God's Spirit that takes place only in regenerate persons. Counseling, therefore, must be seen as a part of the sanctification process. But no one can be sanctified until and unless he has first been regenerated and justified. Changes made by unbelievers are displeasing to God, even when formally in accordance with His Word, because they are but skin deep. They do not stem from a heart of love for Jesus Christ. They are hypocritical: outward only. God did not command His church to make hypocrites (those whose outer state does not conform to their inner one). There are enough whitewashed sepulchers, full of death and corruption within. We do not need to manufacture more.

What then should you do? Certainly not attempt to do the impossible—counsel unbelievers. Instead, do what God commanded in the first place: evangelize them! That does not mean you should not do good for unbelievers—feeding, clothing them—but it does mean that you should not attempt to make *them* do good. That is something, as we have seen, they are incapable of doing. Because some have misunderstood this important distinction, they have confused two very different matters.

How does the counselor go about evangelizing unregenerate persons? After listening to their problems and clarifying the issues involved in them, he may say something like this: "Your difficulties are serious. Indeed, they are so serious that there is no way for you or me to remedy them. Only God can do that. God has the solution to every one of the problems you presented. But there is just one thing—the answers are on the other side of the wall. Before you can have access to them, you must learn how to get over there where the answers are found. There is only one way to get to the other side of the wall, and that is through the door—Jesus Christ (John 10:9). Let's talk about that." Obviously all sorts of other illustrations may be used, but in this one you have a basic paradigm.

It is not only a waste of time to attempt to change unbelievers since any change they make is other than the change that God requires, but it is positively harmful to try. Because unbelievers who follow your advice and make outward changes receive a small amount of relief, they may think they have the real thing. That is a twofold tragedy. First, they settle for something other than God's way while thinking that they have actually pleased Him. This makes it harder for them to recognize their need for a Savior. Those who think they are well do not call for the doctor. And secondly, since the change they make is superficial and does not go to the heart of the matter, in six weeks or six months it will fall apart. Then, thinking that they tried God's counsel (even though they didn't), they will conclude, "God's way doesn't work either." Either way, you have harmed the potential counselee.

It is strange to see pastors who in the pulpit declare, "God didn't send me here to reform you, but to preach a message that will transform you," take off their preaching caps, put on their counseling caps, and go from the pulpit to the study to—**reform** counselees! The inconsistency is glaring, but many fail to see it. Chapter two of I Corinthians, understood and applied to Christian counseling ought to open their eyes.

As you can see from the way in which I have been handling the first two chapters of I Corinthians, there is quite a different approach in this volume from the average commentary. That certainly does not mean that I am finding fault with them, but it does mean that there is something more to be discovered from such an analysis. Like other commentators, I have attempted to understand the flow of the passage in question. But beyond that I have done two other things: 1) I have been interested in the implications of the truths taught for Christian counseling. As you begin to see, there are many. 2) I have been concerned also not only with what Paul wrote (much of that, found in the standard commentaries, I have left out), but particularly with how the Holy Spirit guided him to write it. Approach, words, care in qualifying one's self, etc., are all matters about which the inspiring Holy Spirit had a deep concern and about which counselors ought also to be vitally concerned. Far less has been said about such matters elsewhere, and yet they should be of the greatest moment to the Christian counselor. Perhaps by now you are beginning to understand— and, I hope, appreciate—my methodology. As you read, remember, keep looking for two things: *content*, and how it applies to biblical counseling; *approach*, how Paul, under God's Spirit, deals with the Corinthians' problems.

CHAPTER 3

1 Yet, brothers, I wasn't able to speak to you as to spiritual persons, but as to fleshly ones—as babies in Christ.

2 I gave you milk, not food, because you weren't ready for it yet. Indeed, you still aren't ready.

3 You still are fleshly. When there is jealousy and strife among you, aren't you behaving like fleshly people; aren't you walking like men without the Spirit?

4 Whenever one says, "I am of Paul," and another, "I am of Apollos," aren't you like such men?

At the end of the previous chapter Paul declared, "We have the mind of Christ." That might be misunderstood to mean that all of the thinking and decision-making of a Christian is correct—even, as New Agers aver, divine. Paul will not for a moment allow any such misunderstanding. The Corinthians have been doing much wrong thinking that has lead to much wrong living. Following on immediately thereafter, in very clear language, he tells them so (vv. 1-4).

The point Paul had been making was that in possessing the Holy Spirit, Who knows the divine mind, Christians have access to divine thinking that others do not. Yet in Corinth they were acting as though nothing of the sort were true: "Aren't you walking like people without the Spirit?" (v. 3b). Paul is not asserting that they are without the Spirit (i.e., were not "spiritual")[1] but that in their ongoing, day-by-day behavior they were living like those who were not Christians.

Some find two categories of *Christians* here: Spiritual and Unspiritual. To do so is to misunderstand Paul. All Christians are spiritual. He has just spent time telling them that that is the fundamental difference between the regenerate and the unregenerate. The former possess the Spirit and are able to accept, comprehend and obey God's Word, "the teachings of God's Spirit" (2:14). The latter cannot do so because they are bereft of the Spirit. To be "spiritual" does not characterize one as a top-of-

---

1. It would have been foolish to expect Christian behavior from those he just finished saying were incapable of it.

5   What then is Apollos? And what is Paul? They are servants through whom you believed, but it was by each one only as the Lord appointed:
6   I planted, Apollos watered; but it was God Who brought about the growth.

---

the-totem-pole type Christian, but simply as a Christian: "If anyone doesn't have God's Spirit, he doesn't belong to him" (Romans 8:9).*

Paul found it hard to talk to them as Christians, however; their lives were so substandard (v. 1). He almost had to treat them as unbelievers ("fleshly"; carnal persons, i.e., persons without the Spirit). Because they were Christians, though extremely weak, he calls them "babies in Christ," a figure he carries through in verse two: "I gave you milk, not food, because you weren't ready for it. Indeed, still you aren't ready" (v. 2).

To understand the passage you must see that Paul recognized but two categories of persons: spiritual (all Christians) and carnal [fleshly] (non-Christians). The trouble he describes is that *although they did have the Spirit* (i.e., were "spiritual," or Spirit-possessing persons) they acted so much like unbelievers he wasn't able to talk to them as he wanted to about "the deep thoughts of God" (2:10). He had to treat them like brand-new converts.

Verses 1 and 2 exhibit a concern that some miss: *in counseling, not everyone may be treated alike.* There are degrees of readiness in accepting biblical teaching and living in accordance with it (v. 2: "...you aren't ready"). Paul's language in verse 1 (lit., "I wasn't able to speak to you as spiritual persons") and in verse 2 ("you weren't yet ready for it, indeed, still you aren't ready") is strong. Every counselor, therefore, must evaluate the readiness of his counselee to hear and live truth. This is no excuse for failure to obey God, and Paul did not hesitate to teach them what they needed to know and insist on their doing it throughout the remainder of the epistle. However in this very long letter not only does he find it necessary to discuss many different problems but also to do so, often, in painstaking detail. He must treat them as children who are inexperienced in doing God's will. Because of their spiritual immaturity, in God's providence, in this letter you will find truth given and applied very concretely—just the way your counselee may need to get it.

Counselors who treat all counselees alike err. There are some to whom you may say, "Now you know God expects you to..." and before you can complete your sentence the counselee will probably finish it for you. However this sort of counselee is probably in the minority. Many counselees seek (or are sent to) counseling *because* of the consequences of their ignorance of truth and resultant sinful life-styles. Instead of finding it easy to refer to truths that all spiritual persons alike believe, Paul found it necessary to explain everything in detail as if he were writing to newborn Christians who were hearing it for the first time. You will discover that in counseling you will find yourself, time and again, not only spelling out elementary teachings, but also correcting misinterpretations—even of these! So *never* assume too much knowledge or understanding on the part of your counselee. Always spell things out simply, clearly, and in detail.

Now, notice also (v. 3) that Paul names problems *in biblical terms*: he tells the Corinthians that they are acting like unbelievers ("fleshly" persons) and failing to "walk" (behave, conduct their lives) like people in whom God's Spirit dwells. How does he know that? The divisions among them are proof of it: there is "jealousy and strife." These, as he says elsewhere, are works of the *flesh* (Gal. 5:20).

A large problem in the counseling field is the use of non-biblical labels and other language, particularly the use of euphemisms. For instance, instead of calling sin, "sin" (when it truly is), some counselors will label it "sickness," "immaturity" or "an emotional problem." Labels are not only signs, but also sign posts. They point not merely to the problem, but also to its remedy. If you know the disease, you know what medicine to take. If you call something "sickness," that points to the physician using medicine, rather than to the pastor using the Word of God to solve the problem. If you label sin "immaturity" (other than as a figure of speech), there is little to do about it except sit around and wait for a person to grow up! If you speak of sin as "an emotional problem" you either treat it chemically or with shock therapy, because emotions cannot be reached *directly* in any other way. However there is no emotional problem at all; the counselee's emotions are working perfectly—otherwise he would not be feeling so miserable.

Language, then, is important. Yet I find biblically-oriented counselors using psychological jargon all the time. It is a mistake, a gross one—you can't look up "schizophrenia" in Strong's concordance! If, on the other hand, you speak of "jealousy and strife," as Paul does, you can find ample teaching about these two sins in the Scriptures. But if you label them a "personality disorder" or "dysfunctional behavior," you will be unable to discover anything in your concordance about either. Truly biblical counselors are careful to label counselee problems biblically. That means you must know how the Bible describes various sins and other dif-

7   So neither the planter nor the waterer is anything; the only One Who counts is God Who brings about the growth.

8   The planter and the waterer are one, and each will receive his own wages in keeping with his own labor.

9   We are God's co-workers; you are God's field, God's building.

---

ficulties, so that whenever you encounter them you may be able to identify and label them correctly, so far as possible, using biblical terminology. Then both you and your counselee will be able to find God's answer to each difficulty in God's Word. In this instance, for example, not only can you use the passage in I Corinthians, but knowing that "jealousy and strife" were at the bottom of these unholy divisions, you could also turn to James 4:13-18 where he, in discussing jealousy and strife, adds significant information.

In the days in which we are living, age-old human values have been rejected and in their place opposite values have been substituted. "Self-esteem" used to be a derogatory phrase; to say someone has high self-esteem was, in biblical language, to call him "proud" or "arrogant." The evil one, however, has succeeded in making many (among them, even Christians) think high self-esteem is an ideal, a goal to be pursued. That is not how Scripture views the matter. Paul has already said that *no one* should boast in God's presence (1:29). Paul is concerned about the attitude that puts men on a pedestal—it is a "fleshly" one (3:4). No person is above another, he maintains; they are all working together as one (v. 8). And none of them "is anything" (v. 7). Each does what he was called to do as a worker in God's field—one planting, another watering—but "it was God who brought about the growth" (v. 6). Again Paul emphasizes the Lord; His servants are nothing.

In this day of hero worship (of athletes, movie and TV "personalities") the same spirit has seeped into the church, so that, as in Corinth (a center of the Corinthian games), people follow certain preachers and pit them over against one another like athletes. This, Paul says, is carnality. It is born of jealousy and strife and exalts those who are nothing to a place reserved for our Lord Jesus Christ (v. 7).

Often counselees follow men, exalting them, fighting out of jealousy and causing strife in homes and churches. The resolution of such problems is to turn zeal for men and esoteric ideas into zeal for Christ, as Paul does. But care must be taken to see that even this correct emphasis itself is

10 By the grace that God gave me, like a wise master builder, I laid the foundation, but another is building on it. Let each one watch how he builds!

11 There is no other foundation that one can lay than the one that was laid, which is Jesus Christ.

12 Now if somebody builds on the foundation with gold, silver, valuable gems, wood, hay, stubble,

13 each one's work will become apparent; the Day will show what it is, because it will be revealed by fire. By testing, the fire will demonstrate what sort of work each one has done.

14 The one whose work remains on the foundation will receive his wages.

15 The one whose work is burned up will lose them; he himself will be saved, yet only as someone who has escaped through the fire.

---

not turned into an occasion for piousity and strife; remember those who said: "I am of Christ" (1:12).

Following the previous discussion, Paul's use of an illustration ("you are... God's building," v. 9) leads to an important warning: "Let each one watch how he builds!" (v. 10b). While it is true that Paul, Apollos and Peter work in concert, there is the possibility of others at work as well (II Corinthians indicates how timely this warning was). Wherever he went, Paul's steps were dogged by legalistic Judaizers who sought to wean his converts away from him. He knew that, sooner or later, the Corinthian church would be assailed.

God's temple is being built by God's workers for God's glory to be inhabited by God's Spirit (cf. 3:16, 17; 6:19; II Cor. 6:16). The temple is God's people (v. 17). Divisions among God's people were hurting temple construction; if they allowed true teachers to capture their attention so as to harm the building of the church, wouldn't they be likely to become enamored with false teachers if and when they appeared?

Paul is wise to warn beforehand. Of course, that had been God's way *from the Garden*. Adam and Eve were warned before they fell, the people entering the land were warned at Mt. Ebal; that is how God operates. So should His servants. So must you, as a counselor. When you see the possibility of a counselee open to influences destructive to God's work, it is your duty to sketch out the possibility along with its consequences. This Paul does in verses 10-17.

There are many interesting elements in these seven verses that might be explored, but commentators do a fairly good job at that. Instead, the preventive nature of his words is for our purposes, most significant.

16 Don't you know that you are God's temple, and that God's Spirit dwells in you?

17 If anybody destroys God's temple, God will destroy him, because God's temple is holy (and you are that temple).

18 Stop kidding yourselves; whoever among you thinks that he is wise by modern standards, let him become a fool so that he may become wise.

19 This world's wisdom with God is foolishness (as it is written: **He catches the wise by their own schemes**;

It is clear that Paul is speaking of those who will minister to the Corinthians after he laid the foundation of the church. That foundation, which was Christ (v. 11), is solid. Upon it he wants to see erected a fine temple of a quality that will last eternally (gold, silver, gems [or costly stones]), not one that will be destroyed when God tests it (one built of wood, hay, stubble) at the judgment (vv. 12-14). And the one who builds poorly, if a believer, will, like someone fleeing from a burning building, barely escape with only his life. He will carry nothing with him (no "wages," v. 14). His works will all be burned up (v. 15). More severely, Paul warns, "If anyone destroys God's Temple, God will destroy him" (v. 17). The word translated "destroy" (*pheiro*) has as its basic idea "to make worse, mar, or injure" (Hodge). The penalty for harming the physical temple was death (Lev. 15:31) or expulsion (Num. 19:20). Teaching divisive doctrine harmed God's temple (the church). Warning is God's way. Counselors must not hesitate to use proper, biblical warnings whenever appropriate.

Paul moves on to the problem of self-deception (v. 18). Anyone who thinks he is wise by modern, worldly standards (whatever they may be at any given time) deceives himself. How many Christians who counsel are proud of their worldly learning! And it is these same persons, as a result, who have flooded the church (to its harm) with all sorts of psychological wood, hay and stubble under the rubrics of "God's truth." Take warning, Christian counselor, how you build, i.e., what you teach your counselees (and you do teach, even by refusing to teach)! The way to become "wise" in God's eyes is to become a fool in the world's sight by teaching and counseling according to Scripture (vv. 18-23). It is crucial too for a counselor to finally come to a realization that the teaching of the Word by all of God's servants is "all yours" (v. 21).

This leads to one more observation: by choosing one leader to the exclusion of others the Corinthians had limited their options. When it comes to the acquisition of truth, God has provided abundantly for all counseling needs (II Timothy 3:17). We have a very large resource base

20 and again: **The Lord knows how useless the reasoning of the wise is**).

21 So let no one boast about human beings; everything is yours:

22 whether it is Paul or Apollos or Cephas, or whether it is the world or life or death, or the present or the future; they are all yours,

23 and you are Christ's and Christ is God's.

---

from which to draw (v. 21, 22). Indeed, in that base Christ Himself is included (v. 23). So why adopt an either/or attitude when within Biblical parameters there is such large scope? Teach counselees, who are narrower than Paul, the importance of a both/and approach to truth. There is the possibility of learning even from brothers in other denominations with whom we may have serious disagreement. Usually *something* (however small) they know, do, think is closer to Scripture than you or your counselee know or do. Divisions among believers that totally separate them, are unfortunate, because they tend to bring about opposition, pride and contention that harms God's church and truncates one's options for learning. If you were "for Paul" and "against Apollos and Peter," your ability to learn from all God's resource persons would have been reduced two-thirds.

CHAPTER 4

1 As for us, let people think of us as Christ's attendants and stewards of God's mysteries.
2 The key thing that is sought in stewards is that they be found faithful.
3 To me it is of little consequence to be judged by you or by the judgment of any other human being; indeed, I don't even judge myself.
4 Now I am not conscious of anything against myself, but that doesn't mean that I am innocent. The One Who judges me is the Lord.

Yes, as Paul said, "Everything is yours" (3:21), and "you are Christ's and Christ is God's" (3:23). Then Paul urges, "...let people think of us [Paul, Apollos, etc.] as Christ's attendants [lit., 'underrowers'; cf. Acts 13:5] and stewards [i.e., guardians and dispensers] of God's mysteries." An "attendant" or "assistant" is someone who takes orders from another—simply put, one who is in the *service* of God.

The only thing that really counts in a steward is that he be found faithful to the one whose property he manages. God, then, is the One to Whom a minister of the Word must answer: it is by Him he will be judged (v. 2). So Paul really didn't care what others thought of him as a minister (that, of course, is not the same as saying he wasn't concerned about how he affected people). He was no pleaser of men. Untold agony is suffered by those who regularly court the good opinion of others. It is an idolatry that displaces Jesus Christ and places others on His throne. And saddest of all, it is an impossibility. Counselees need to cultivate Paul's relaxed attitude toward others, all the while seeking to please Jesus alone. Neither the Corinthians nor any other human being could truly evaluate his work and, in particular, his motives. In fact he didn't even trust his own judgment of himself (v. 3). He could not be sure, even though he was not conscious of anything against himself, that he was entirely innocent; motives are tricky (v. 4).

It is important not to try to judge motives. When approaching motives you should always take warning. Yet some counselors try to evaluate another's heart (inner values, motives, thinking, etc.). All such should read I Samuel 16:7, and Paul's word here: "The One who judges me is the Lord" (v. 4). The **Lord** is the Heartknower. No man can know another's heart. Counselors have no right to deal with anything but what they hear

5   So don't judge ahead of time, before the Lord comes, Who will bring to light the things that are now hidden in darkness and will make the purposes of hearts to appear. At that time each one will receive his praise from God.

6 Now these things I have applied figuratively to myself and to Apollos for your sakes, brothers, in order that you may learn from us not to go beyond what has been written, so that you may not proudly set up one teacher against a different one.

---

and see (the outward appearance belongs to you; the heart to God alone).

We must judge, of course, but judgment must be righteous, unbiased (cf. Mt. 7:1ff. with John 7:24). Our judgments of others always must be qualified, and often tentative, since they are based on outer factors alone.

Of importance, too, is the fact that—unlike some counselees who become too introspective—Paul didn't sit around judging his *own* motives. He recognized how self-deceptive one can be even in this. To those caught in this trap (and it is likely that you will see them sooner rather than later in counseling), refer them to verses 3-5: "I don't even judge myself" (3), "the One who judges me is the Lord" (4), "So don't judge ahead of time" (5). Paul left all heart judgment—even judgment of the inner Paul—to the Lord at His coming. Motives are such a mixed bag. Counselees bogged down in the mire of introspection must be told that they are attempting to steal God's prerogative of judging motives from Him and should be urged to stop doing so. At His coming the wrong motives of ministry, hidden in darkness, will be revealed so that at last we shall know our hearts (v. 5). And those things that are good and proper will be made apparent as God praises the one who was trustworthy: "Well done, you good and faithful servant."

Paul wants the Corinthians to "learn from" himself and the other apostles (v. 6). He says that he had worked out principles they need to know, using himself and Apollos as examples. The Corinthians, childlike as they were (in spite of their supposed sophistication), needed to see the principles applied—even if done so hypothetically. Children learn largely by example. Many counselees will not understand biblical principles or know how to apply them to life until you "show" the principles at work in examples. The counselor, *perhaps even more than the preacher*, must become good at developing and using illustrations of truth. The idea of learning by example comes up frequently in Scripture. We shall reserve a full discussion of it till chapter 11:1, one *locus classicus*.

His chief concern is finally summed up by Paul in verse 6: "...so that you may not boastfully set up one teacher against another." Paul lays

7   Who makes you different? And what do you have that you didn't receive? Indeed, if you received it, why do you boast as if you didn't receive it?

8 Are you already filled to satisfaction? Have you already become rich? Are you reigning without us? I wish you really were reigning so that we too were reigning with you!

9   It appears that God has exhibited us apostles at the tail end of the triumphal procession like those prisoners who are doomed to death, because we have become a spectacle to the world, both to angels and to human beings.

10 We are fools for Christ's sake, but you are smart in Christ! We are weak, but you are strong! You are famous, but we are infamous!

11 Right up to this moment we go hungry and thirsty, we are naked and slapped around and wander about homeless,

---

down a very important command: do not "go beyond what is written." The cause of the difficulty was abandoning scriptural principles for teachings "beyond." This, indeed, is a very prevalent problem today, not only for counselees who thereby get into trouble, but for counselors who look outside of Scripture for answers. Legalism is, fundamentally, adding humanly-devised rules to Scriptural injunctions.

The thought of boasting brings up another: why do people boast anyway? Different excellencies found among teachers are from God, and everything worthwhile they have to offer was "received" by grace. All the glory, for anything profitable, goes to God.

At this point Paul turns to cutting irony: "So," he says, "you [babies] think you are way ahead of the rest of us? You are already on the throne? And we apostles have become like prisoners at the tail-end of a Roman triumphal procession, a spectacle to everyone? We are weak, infamous fools for Christ's sake, but you are strong, famous and smart? Is that how you see things? Well then," Paul continues, right up to the moment of writing, "it is true, we do go hungry and naked, are often homeless and insulted, persecuted and treated as scum. But remember, all of this is for Christ's sake."

Irony may be (often must be) used to break down pride and arrogance in counselees. Paul was good at it, as you can see here. These words were calculated to hit hard and, from the results evident in II Corinthians, had salutary effects. When should you use it? Whenever the absurdity of a counselee's viewpoint (or action) cannot be made apparent to him in any other way.

12 and we labor with our own hands. When we are insulted, we bless; when persecuted, we endure.

13 When we are defamed, we gently appeal; until now we have become like the world's filth, the scum of all sorts of people!

14 I am not writing these things to shame you, but to counsel you as my dear children.

15 Even if you have ten thousand guardians in Christ, you cannot have many fathers. Now in Christ Jesus it was I who fathered you by the good news.

16 I urge you, then, become imitators of me.

17 For this very reason I sent Timothy to you. He, my dear and faithful child in the Lord, will remind you of my ways in Christ Jesus, which are in agreement with what I teach everywhere in every church.

18 Some are acting arrogantly, as if I weren't going to come to you,

---

Then comes verse 14, a verse mentioned in the introduction of this book. Paul's irony had been sharp, as it needed to be, but again he is careful to note that his *ultimate* purpose was not to "shame" them (but if shame led to repentance, okay); his purpose was pastoral. By nouthetic confrontation he sought to bring about change for their benefit, out of love for them as his "dear children" (converts). The cutting edge of his irony is like a surgeon's scalpel. He hurts, only in order to heal.

The familial note now prevails (vv. 15-17): "I am your Father in the Faith" (the one who first preached the gospel to you and therefore has the loving concerns of a father for you). He is appealing to the warm relationship that once existed between them. "Be imitators of me" (just as children imitate their fathers). I sent Timothy, who will remind you of your spiritual father's ways, so that you can. And please note, what I am teaching you I teach in every church: I'm not laying some special burden on you! Sometimes it is helpful to use printed handouts in counseling, especially for homework, since these indicate what one is requiring is a standard procedure.

In verses 18-21, Paul shows how his fatherly concern exhibited itself in relationship to them. Some said Paul was all talk and no action, that he said he'd come to Corinth and didn't. The attitudes of some toward their spiritual father could be called nothing short of "arrogant" (vv. 18, 19). So he lets them know that is precisely what he thinks of them! Think about **that**! Surely from time to time you have thought so about a counselee. Did you tell him so? That, too, is a part of biblical counseling. Sometimes the only honest appraisal a counselee will ever receive is from you—don't you owe it to him when he needs to hear it?

19 but I will come to you soon, if the Lord wills, and I will learn not only about the talk of these arrogant people but also about their power!
20 God's empire isn't characterized by talk but by power.
21 Which do you want—shall I come to you with a rod, or with love and a spirit of meekness?

I will come as soon as Christ wills (v. 19) and we'll see who is all talk and who has power! God operates among His people in power, not in mere talk (cf. Romans 14:17). I have refrained from coming because I would have had to come with a rod in my hand. I'm giving you an opportunity to clean up your act so I can come, when I do, in a loving spirit of meekness. That, in a nutshell, is Paul's response.

God wants results, not mere talk. The same counselor and the same counselees, at various times, require different approaches. There are two sides to all counseling: a rodlike side and the opposite. Every counselor must have both in his repertoire. Some men are too limited, stressing only one side or the other. Love, like fatherly action, demands both. How extensive is your counseling? Could it be that when counseling fails it is sometimes because you are afraid to "tell it like it is?"

But remember, all of this strong language is the language of a father to his disobedient children (v. 14). The mention of the "rod" of discipline (v. 21) shows that his reprimands are well-intended—not merely outbursts of a scorned and bitter teacher. No, good counseling can never be that. Even scolding (as we see is sometimes necessary) must be done out of a caring, fatherly approach.

CHAPTER 5

1 It is generally reported that there is sexual immorality among you, and sexual immorality of a sort that isn't found among the Gentiles—that someone has his father's wife.
2 You are arrogant! Shouldn't you rather have mourned, and removed from your midst the one who has done this thing?

Paul has just called some of the Corinthians "arrogant" (see the last chapter). He did not hesitate to use plain-spoken language when it was appropriate. Counselors must learn to do so too, when it is accurate and when what they say is calculated to bring counselees to their senses. Once again he says it: "You are arrogant" (5:2). But now, the accusation seems to be universal. In 4:18 it was "some" that he considered "arrogant"; now there is no such qualification. Why the difference? Well, the previous discussion had to do with a personal attack by some upon Paul. "He's all talk and no action," they were saying. Presumably this was not the opinion of the majority. But now he turns his attention to a matter that did involve the entire congregation. The Corinthian Church was actually allowing a case of known incest to continue undisciplined. Why would Paul think that "arrogant?"

The accusation was fitting because they must have thought themselves able to live with and above the sin, unaffected. Presumably something of that nature led to pride, because they actually "boasted" about it (v. 6). Others might be contaminated, *they would not.* "Oh?" asks Paul, "Don't you know that a little leaven leavens the whole lump?" This boasting that they were immune to the effects of evil in their midst was what led Paul to charge them with arrogance. And rightly so! That sort of pride "leads to destruction." They must take heed "lest they fall." The person who lifts himself to a pinnacle sways with the wind and is always in danger of falling off. The very same problem may be found in many counselees. Tolerating sin of all sorts they think they will be unaffected by it, when all the time, weak as they are, they are in danger of sliding into the same sin themselves.

There is a good bit to learn about counseling from chapter five. For one thing, public, scandalous sin is the responsibility of the whole church. No one can shake off his responsibility by asking, "Am I my brother's

3   Even though I am absent in the body, I am present in the spirit and, as if I were present, have already made a judgment about the one who has been doing this thing.

4   When you are assembled, and my spirit and the power of our Lord Jesus are with you, in the Name of the Lord Jesus

5   deliver this person to Satan for the destruction of the flesh so that his spirit may be saved on the Lord's Day.

---

keeper?" The answer to that is "absolutely!" The sinful actions of the member of the church who had his father's wife (probably his stepmother) were a clear violation of Leviticus 18:8. He was living with her in fornication (to "have" means to *live with sexually*; cf. John 4:18). Incidentally, this is one of those places that show the broad scope of the word "fornication." It is used in the Bible to speak of any and all sorts of sexual sin (see also Jude 7).

Note that this sin was publicly known ("It is generally reported"). That is, it was scandalous, particularly since it was the sort of sin, as Paul does not fail to mention, that was abhorred even by pagan gentiles (v. 1). Paul had heard about the sin from any number of persons. In cases where sin is scandalous and unrepented of, it may (must) be dealt with formally at the level of the church without proceeding first through the earlier steps of discipline required in Matthew 18:15ff. This very week I received a phone call from a pastor trying to exercise biblical discipline toward someone in another church with the matter fully known to members of both congregations. But the minister of the second church refused to act because the parties concerned had not gone through the informal steps of church discipline. This matter was every bit as "commonly known" and, therefore, scandalous as the matter in Corinth. Either the second minister was conveniently using this response as a ploy for not becoming involved or he is sadly lacking in his understanding of church discipline. The matter was no more a personal matter, between two parties that had to proceed from a one-on-one confrontation to telling it "to the church," than was the matter in Corinth. Note carefully, Paul does not refer to earlier steps of discipline; when the matter is scandalous it must be dealt with at the level at which it is known.

No one should be put out of the church because of his sin (as though some sins require discipline and others do not). No, precisely not that. It is, as Matthew 18 indicates, at every point, the failure to "hear" that moves discipline on to the next stage and ultimately to the final act of putting one out of the midst. If upon proper admonition, however, one repents and begins to live as he should, he should remain within the body of believers.

It is important to observe that, while in no way excusing the Corinthian offender's sin, Paul is harder on the smug Corinthian church than he is on the man committing incest. How many churches have been weakened by allowing the continued, unrepentant membership of persons involved in scandalous sins! Christ's Name has been smeared in the dirt by such failure. Members have become lax in their own living, thinking "Well, if they aren't doing anything about Paul or Mildred, then surely they won't get after me." Whenever confronted by scandalous situations—and if you are doing effective counseling you will be—you must be clear and firm about the biblical requirements. Your counsel could make all the difference. But it means also that you must thoroughly understand the many details of church discipline and, when necessary, insist on its use as Paul did. There will be times when congregations, out of a superior attitude that Paul described as "arrogant," themselves must be strongly rebuked.

What is the proper action in scandalous cases? First the goal is to convict the offender of his sin by confronting him with appropriate Scripture, calling on him to repent. If he does, rejoice! A brother has been reclaimed. He then must be restored to full fellowship as indicated in II Corinthians 2:7, 8 (the process of restoration will be described in that place).

But if he refuses to repent, as in the case in I Corinthians, then the congregation should 1) "mourn" over the fact, beseeching God for him, and 2) put him out of the church. That does not mean to physically exclude him from listening to the preaching of the Word (you don't do that to others considered unbelievers), but it means he is no longer under the care and discipline of the church. Instead, he is "handed over" ("delivered") to Satan. That is to say, he is now considered "*as* a heathen and a tax collector." He is outside the protection and benefits of Christ's church. Satan may now deal with him in ways in which he could not when he was still protected by membership in Christ's organized church. This rough handling by Satan is calculated to destroy "the flesh" (v. 5). There are two possible meanings of those words: either that Satan is permitted to afflict him physically, as he is forbidden to afflict a Christian (I John 5:18), or Satan's dealings with him will bring him to his senses, thus destroying the flesh (his sinful habit patterns). The former explanation, rather than the latter, seems slightly more likely to be the true one. Either way, handing

6   Your boasting is no good. Don't you know that a little leaven leavens the whole lump?

7   Clean out the old leaven so that you may be a new unleavened lump, as in fact you are. Christ, our Passover Lamb, has been sacrificed.

8   So then, let us keep the feast not with old leaven, nor with leaven of malice and evil, but with the unleavened bread of sincerity and truth.

---

an unrepentant sinner over to Satan is designed not merely to rid the church of his influence, but also as the final attempt to reclaim him.

Today, when someone is "removed from the midst" (v. 2) he frequently runs down the street to the next church on the block which welcomes him with open arms. It is a serious sin on the part of that church to fail to recognize and respect the rightly-handled discipline of the previous one. It virtually means, you should point out to that church, that logically the second congregation is either calling the disciplining congregation a non-church or it considers itself a synagogue of Satan (since the person put out is delivered over to Satan)! Either way, serious problems arise, into which a good counselor will always interpose himself to attempt to rearrange matters biblically.

In verses 3 and 4, Paul asserts the apostolic authority given to him by Christ when he declares that he already has judged the issue and (in spirit, though not able to be physically present) will be with them, lending apostolic sanction to the removal of the unrepentant offender. The authority he asserts is a derived one, now given to the church to exercise in conjunction with the commands of Scripture. It is Christ's own authority: "in the Name of the Lord Jesus" (v. 4).

One reason for the removal of the offender, we saw, is to bring him to repentance (v. 5). In this case it worked, as we shall see when studying II Corinthians 2. Another reason is to disinfect the church (vv. 6-8). Paul makes this point in terms of the Passover, at which time all leaven was removed from the midst, thereby symbolizing that all of Egypt (the past life of slavery to sin) has been cleaned out. Paul drives home this point in verse 8 by extending the figure, also calling the leaven "malice" and "evil." This he applies not only to the incestuous brother, but to the various sins of others in the congregation. In his typical put-on-to-replace what is put-off-to-remove fashion, Paul urges the Corinthians to "sincerity and truth."

Now, in verses 9-13, Paul writes generally about sexual sin among believers and unbelievers, and how non-sinning Christians should relate to both.

9 I wrote to you in my letter not to get mixed up with those who are sexually immoral;

10 not that you shouldn't have anything whatever to do with the sexually immoral of this world (or with greedy persons, or robbers, or idolaters) since to do that you would have to leave the world altogether.

11 But now let me explain that what I wrote was that you must not get mixed up with any so-called brother who is sexually immoral, or greedy, or an idolater, or a slanderer, or a drunkard or a robber; you must not even eat with a person like that.

12 What reason would I have to judge those who are outside? Isn't it those who are inside that you are to judge?

13 God will judge those who are outside. Get this wicked person out of your midst!

Paul reminds his readers of the directions he gave them in a previous letter (v. 9): "not to get mixed up with those who are sexually immoral." The statement is qualified—"I don't mean that you shouldn't have *anything* to do with immoral unbelievers, or that would mean leaving the world altogether (v. 10). Naturally you must buy, etc., from the greedy, idolatrous, sexually-sinful people around you in the course of ordinary life. That isn't what I forbade. Indeed, I was speaking particularly about mingling with 'so-called' Christians who are living immorally" (v. 11). Here Paul is concerned with persons, still members of the church, who are under discipline by the church (cf. II Thessalonians 3:14, 15). Normal relations, "mingling," are not proper. Eating, shopping together, playing golf, etc., as though nothing were the matter, should be out of the question. In a sense, Paul is more stringent about the relationship to Christians under discipline than to unbelieving sinners. That is natural, because more can be expected of believers. Every counselor must keep this matter in clear focus since it has many implications. Can you think of a few?

If a believer who is under discipline by his church calls another who is not and says, "John, let's go fishing next Saturday," John should reply in this vein: "Tom, I'd love to, but, you see, things are not right. You are under discipline, and remain unrepentant. That puts a space between us. I'd be happy, however, to meet with you to talk about your sin and repentance next Saturday." After all, when taken seriously, Christian relationships do suffer from a brother's failure to repent. Things cannot be normal. Surely you, as a counselor, are going to find yourself instructing many Christians about these matters.

Many times Christians join causes and spend time and money trying to reform a world that will not be reformed. That is not their business, says Paul. I'll leave the unbeliever to God (v. 12). But while you must not judge outsiders, you are obligated to judge those *in* the church. Then in a final, directive command, he orders, "Get this wicked person out of your midst!" (v. 13). Paul's counseling, you will note, has been directive and authoritative all along, but surely here those elements are underlined. Much more about church discipline, in detail, systematically presented, may be found in my book, *A Handbook of Church Discipline* (Zonder-van).

CHAPTER 6

1 When one has a matter against another, how dare any of you take it before unjustified men for judgment rather than before saints?

2   Don't you know that the saints will judge the world? And if the world is to be judged by you, are you incompetent to make judgments about petty matters?

3   Don't you know that we shall judge angels, not to mention matters concerning the everyday affairs of this life?

Abruptly, it seems, Paul turns to the matter of Christians taking one another to court. But when you realize that he has been talking about the church's relationship to unbelievers over against its relationship to erring believers in verses 10-12, the transition does not seem so harsh after all. Since the courts are conducted by unbelievers, clearly the matter of hanging out the church's dirty wash before them was an issue with similar overtones.

Paul is scandalized over the thought of Christians suing Christians and, in addition, doing so before unbelievers. He will take up *both* of those issues. He asks, "How dare you...!" It is not that Paul is idealistic or naive that he does not expect problems—even serious ones—to arise between Christians. No, not that. What scandalized him was that the Corinthians were not resolving these problems *in the church.* Paul's words here are essentially a call for counseling. Such counsel would usually be done by those who are called as a part of their function as elders to watch over the flock. But Paul ranges even more widely, implying that calling on almost anyone in the church would be preferable to bringing matters before unbelieving judges. People who fail to appreciate the counseling role of believers among themselves should be instructed in these words. One can almost hear him saying, "How dare you take your problems before unbelieving counselors and psychologists! Even going to the least brother among you for help would be better than that!"

In this passage, note several things. First, it isn't wrong to want justice; it is perfectly right to take an otherwise unresolved matter before "saints" (v. 1). It is entirely wrong, however, to take another Christian to court before unbelievers. "You will judge angels" (an interesting hint about the future), says the apostle. "Can't you find among you those who

4   So then, when you do have matters that concern the everyday affairs of this life, why do you appoint as judges those who are of no account to the church?

5   I am ashamed to have to say this to you! Could it be that there isn't a single person among you who is wise enough to be able to decide between brothers?

6   Instead, brother goes with brother to be judged before unbelievers!

7   Now, indeed, there is something altogether wrong with you that you even conduct lawsuits against one another—why aren't you rather willing to suffer injustice? Why aren't you rather willing to be deprived of something?

---

are competent to judge one another about the everyday affairs that occasion differences?" he asks (vv. 2, 3). That Paul was restricting his discussion to taking marriage and sexual problems to law, as some think (see Bernard), is in error. This is clear from the general statement about the "everyday affairs of life" (v. 3). In that, there is no such limitation.

Secondly, note, while it is a disgrace to bring the unsolved problems of believers before unbelievers who have not even solved the main question of human existence, that is not all Paul wants you to think about. The very fact that Christians would conduct law suits against other Christians is wrong (v. 7). Paul maintains that Christians should resolve matters between themselves whenever they can, but if they can't, then he asks, "Why not take it on the chin?" (v. 7). Peacemaking is more important than "getting justice." That is what Paul teaches. This is hard for many Christians to fathom because they have become so dreadfully self-centered, but it is an important weapon in the counselor's arsenal to bring forth whenever all attempts at reaching justice have failed. Many a situation can be resolved by one Christian backing down on a *demand* for "justice."

Thirdly, note, Paul makes the point that it is better to suffer than to cause suffering, to be treated unjustly than to act unjustly (v. 8). This is often what happens when one, demanding justice, prosecutes his case strongly against another. He ultimately ends up treating the other more harshly than he himself was treated.

These three principles are of great importance to the Christian counselor. More often than not, he finds himself in the role of peacemaker, even when peacemaking is incidental to other problems. The principles speak for themselves. Narrow, niggardly attitudes have no place in Christ's church. Having one's way, insisting on his rights, demanding justice and taking vengeance are all ways foreign to Christianity.

8   But, instead, you are acting unjustly and depriving others, and you are doing this even to brothers.

9 Don't you know that the unrighteous won't inherit God's empire? Don't be misled—neither those who are sexually immoral, nor idolaters, nor adulterers, nor male prostitutes, nor homosexuals,

10   nor thieves, nor greedy persons, nor drunkards, nor slanderers, nor robbers will inherit God's empire.

11   These are what some of you were. But you were washed, you were sanctified, you were justified in the Name of the Lord Jesus Christ and by the Spirit of our God.

Among the Jews, one did not have to go to law to obtain a divorce; a simple bill of divorcement, in view of witnesses, could be handed to a marriage partner. Today, in our society, divorces are obtained *only by means of going to law before unbelievers*. Therefore, *Christians may not divorce other Christians, because they may not take them to court*. This means that marital problems among Christians must be resolved among the "saints." Few things are more messy than a divorce. Few things grieve Christ more than to see His people unwilling to resolve problems in the home. The believer should be an example to the world in this matter, rather than allowing the world to set the example for him. All true believers have the resources (the Word, the Spirit and the Church) to resolve every problem. They possess all things necessary for life and godliness. It is only when one partner, refusing at all stages of church discipline to hear the church, is put out of the church that he can be taken before the law to obtain a divorce. Only then, when this partner has become "as a heathen and a publican" (Matthew 18:17—i.e., as an unbeliever, outside the church), may this party be divorced (cf. I Corinthians 7:15).

Paul's words in verses 9-11 offer great hope for your counselee. In these verses, he lists many sinful life-styles, life-styles that have become so life-dominating that the person involved can be labeled by the sin that dominates him. But, mercy of mercies, Paul says that by the work of the Savior and the Spirit, persons living that way were justified before God so that in His sight they were considered "holy." He maintains that they were "washed" and "sanctified" putting such things behind them. If God can treat sinners that way, surely fellow-sinners can do the same. Often, homosexuals, drunkards and others will ask counselors if there is any hope of changing. Reading this passage is a powerful response. Paul makes it clear that such things as drunkenness and homosexuality are *not* genetic problems, as some aver, but rather, are sinful life-styles. Life-styles due to genetics do not require forgiveness; but it is also true that

12 All sorts of things are lawful for me, but everything isn't advantageous. All sorts of things are lawful for me, but I won't be ruled by any of them.
13 "Food is for the stomach and the stomach is for food"—true, but God will destroy both of them.
14 But the body is not for sexual immorality but for the Lord, and the Lord for the body—but God raised the Lord and will raise us through His power.

---

they cannot be changed by it either! All the life-styles mentioned here are sin-engendered. The hope lies in this: Jesus Christ died for sins, not for genetic problems. Call what the Bible labels "sin", "sin," and you will restore hope to many who have been led astray by modern propaganda (often disseminated by avant-garde elements in the church itself).

Two key counseling principles may be found in verse 12, each of which puts some restrictions on one's Christian liberty. Christian liberty is *liberty with limits*. The first principle is that things perfectly lawful in themselves are not always advantageous (to the church, others or one's self). Therefore the question is not only "Is it lawful?" but, additionally, one must ask, "If lawful, is it advantageous?" In this, one may see the same spirit that moved Paul to write what he did earlier in the chapter. It is "lawful" to seek justice, but if it is not *advantageous* to Christ's work, it is wrong to insist on doing so. Insisting on one's rights to the point of splitting a congregation, for instance, is always wrong.

The second principle is that one must avoid becoming enslaved to anything that in itself is otherwise lawful. Sex, food, possessions, computers are all lawful. But when one becomes so attached to something that it becomes an idol to him, he has violated the principle and has sinned. To be "ruled" by anyone or anything but Jesus Christ is idolatry. Many of your counselees, who would loudly protest that they are not idolaters ("like those people who worship statues"), need to be shown the basic idolatry in their lives. Idolatry is deceptive; as a result, counselors must be ready to expose it wherever they find it.

Paul discusses fornication in verses 13-20—one such idolatry that rules many in our culture today. He begins by quoting a saying that was in vogue in his day (it sounds a lot like our bumper sticker slogans today): "Food is for the stomach and the stomach is for food." True, he says, but God will destroy both food and stomach (v. 13). The problem was that some were applying the principle lying behind this saying to sexual relations: "As the stomach is designed to handle food, so the body (i.e., its

42

15   Don't you know that your bodies are members of Christ? Shall I therefore take the members of Christ and make them members of a prostitute?
Of course not!

16   Don't you know that the one who is joined to a prostitute becomes one
body with her? "Because," He says, "the two shall become one flesh."

17   But the one who is joined to the Lord becomes one spirit with Him.

18   Flee sexual sin. There are all sorts of sinful things that a person may
do that are outside the body, but the one who commits sexual sin, sins
against his own body.

19   Don't you know that your body is a temple of the Holy Spirit Who is
in you, Whom you have from God? You are not your own,

20   since you were bought with a price; so glorify God in your body.

---

sexual organ) is designed for sexual relations." Therefore, they concluded,
just as we rightly use the stomach to store and assimilate the nutrients in
all sorts of food, we may also legitimately use the body for all sorts of
sexual intercourse. After all, why not, since it was designed for that purpose? "No!" says Paul. The stomach and food will be destroyed, but the
body will be raised up to be Christ's forever (v. 14). From what he says
you might infer that the new bodies in the resurrection will be stomach-
less, but that is not the point of the passage. What Paul is saying is that the
Christian's body is designed to serve the Lord. *That* is its ultimate purpose. God didn't intend the body to be used for sexual sin; He did intend
the stomach to process food. The two ideas are not parallel; you are comparing apples and oranges.

Talking about the body and fornication leads to a valuable discussion
of the same: verses 15-20. The body, bought with the price of Christ's
valuable blood, belongs to Him (v. 20). He has the right to tell your counselee how to use it. When one uses it according to God's directions, he
glorifies God in his body. When he does not, he sins. Feminists, who
claim absolute rights over their bodies, are wrong. You will find counselees infected with such beliefs and must clarify the issue for them. This
passage will be useful in doing so.

A Christian's body, Paul observes, is united to Jesus Christ Who, in
the person of the Holy Spirit, dwells within it. To join this body to a prostitute (v. 15), therefore, is to put Jesus Christ into a blasphemous relationship to that prostitute. They become "one body" (a close union; Paul
won't call it "one flesh," the phrase for a holy union between a man and
wife). He quotes the Genesis passage, however, to show that sexual relations do constitute a close union ("one flesh" is closer than "one body").

43

And the union between Christ and the Christian is closer still: it is a "one spirit" union. In all of this, because of the closeness of Christ to the believer, a Christian may not engage in illicit sexual relations, because to do so is to bring Christ Himself into a sinful union! That is unthinkable!

Temptation in Corinth was strong. Thousands of temple prostitutes roamed the streets plying their trade. This double-seaport city was filled with sailors, travelers and merchants of every sort. It was a fundamentally immoral city. To call someone a "Corinthian" was to insult him by insinuating that he was a bounder. Paul was striking at the heart of society with these words. Yet, even in such a culture, Paul allows no excuses for sexual sin.

Counselors, therefore, must help counselees to "flee" sexual sin. Ways and means of ending illicit sexual alliances and of sustaining a chaste life-style must be thought through, agreed upon by all parties concerned and monitored in counseling so long as the establishment of a new, biblical life-style is in process.

The body is God's temple, Paul reiterates, here referring to the individual's body, as previously he referred to the congregational body (cf. 2:16, 17). This chapter is a powerful tool for use today in our own sex-drenched culture. One additional comment: other sins—murder, theft, etc.—do not affect the body *directly*. But to place one's body into a physical relationship with another exposes it to all sorts of potentially harmful (or even deadly as AIDS has taught us) sexually-transmitted diseases (v. 18). Thus he sins against his own body as well. On all of these counts, Christian counselors are fortified with an armory of weapons for fighting against illegitimate sexual relations. Here is a chapter to be fully understood and frequently quoted in the counseling room.

CHAPTER 7

1 Now, concerning those questions about which you wrote. It is well for a man not to touch a woman.

2   But because of the prevalence of sexual immorality, each man should have his own wife, and each woman should have her own husband.

3 The husband must fulfill his obligation to his wife and the wife also must do the same for her husband.

This is a long chapter that is very important for counselors. It deals with engagement, marriage and sexual relations. Evidently the Corinthians had inquired about some of these issues in a letter (v. 1). Paul begins his answers crisply, "It is well for a man not to touch a woman." That certainly means he should not engage in sexual intercourse with a woman outside of marriage. But it probably goes further, forbidding any and all physical contact. In Corinth, as we have seen, the prostitutes (both male and female), because they were connected with the temple of Aphrodite, offered legitimized fornication. In effect, the Corinthians worshipped sex. Paul refers to this orgiastic milieu by speaking of the "prevalence of sexual immorality."

As an antidote to the problem, Paul stresses the importance of marriage. This solution, he makes clear, is for both men and women (v. 2). Returning to the strong societal temptations that lead to lust within, he also says, "it is better to marry than to burn" (v. 9). So marriage, though not viewed from the highest level as a covenant of companionship, is nevertheless the biblical solution to lust and a safeguard against sexual immorality. You have an obligation to stress this in counseling those struggling with problems of sexual desires. Too often today marriage is put off too long. Because of unbiblical romantic expectations, wrong views of the basis and obligations of marriage, and failure of so many marriages all around, many find it hard to make the commitment. And since our throwaway society is adverse to commitment itself, they find settling down to a one-partner-for-life-obligation, difficult. As a Christian counselor, you must offer Christian solutions to problems. Marriage is the solution to sexual temptation and lust, and you must learn how to overcome objections and hindrances to it.

Within marriage, there are obligations. The great principle in verses 3 and 4 is critical to all marriage counseling. Sexual relations are an equal

4 The wife doesn't have authority over her own body; rather it is her husband who does. Also, the husband doesn't have authority over his own body; rather it is his wife who does.

5 Don't deprive one another, except by agreement for a time that you may devote yourselves to prayer. Then come together again so that Satan may not be able to tempt you because of your lack of self-control.

6 Now I say this as a concession, not as an order.

---

obligation of both parties (v. 3). But in fulfilling the obligation one must do so *lovingly*. Love is giving; lust is demanding something for one's self. Neither marriage partner has authority over his own body; the other party does (v. 4). That means one must not seek his or her own sexual satisfaction, but the satisfaction of one's partner. In a variety of ways, this important principle solves problems. One party says, "I don't get any pleasure out of sexual relations." The answer? "Well, that shouldn't be your goal. It should be to satisfy your partner. And incidentally, that which gives the most pleasure, as a sort of reflex, is knowing you have done so."

In verse 5, Paul observes that it is wrong to withhold sexual satisfaction from one another, except when both agree to it, briefly, in some emergency, to devote themselves to prayer. But even then, at the end of the season of prayer they must come together quickly in sexual relations to avoid any temptation. Withholding sexual intercourse, for whatever other reasons, is sin. Legal separation, for this reason as well as for others, is therefore unbiblical. The Scriptures know nothing of such a thing and here clearly condemn it.

Now Paul enters a discussion not always clearly understood. He says that to urge marriage under present conditions (vv. 26, 29 indicate that a period of great persecution was about to break out) is a "concession" (v. 6). It would be better during a period of intense persecution not to find it necessary to carry the extra burden of marriage. Presumably Paul, being a prophet, was able to predict the Neronian persecution (as did John in the Book of Revelation). But, he says, his statement that "each man should have his own wife, and each woman should have her own husband," being a "concession" to human weakness, is certainly "not...an order" (v. 6b). There are many decisions counselees must make that, since they fall within basic biblical parameters as this one does, are matters of judgment and prudence, according to individual circumstances.

For a counselor to dictate what counselees "must" do under those circumstances is to do what Paul refused to do. It is a legalistic imposition of

7   I wish every person was like myself; but each one has his own gift from God—one of this sort, another of that.

8   To the single men and to the widows I say that it is well for them to remain like me.

9   But if they can't control themselves they must marry, since it is better to marry than to burn.

10   To those who are married I give this authoritative instruction (not I, but the Lord): A wife must not separate from her husband

11   (but if she does indeed separate, she must remain unmarried or be reconciled to her husband); and a husband must not divorce his wife.

---

the counselor's judgment upon his counselee. There is, here, a fine line to observe. On the one hand, Paul does not hesitate to express his own opinion: "I wish every person was like myself" (v. 7a—i.e., single), but on the other, he says, "each one has his own gift from God" (v. 7). Clearly Paul, like Jesus (Matt. 19:10-12), believed some had the gift of singleness, but others did not. This gift is useful in periods of persecution. What it seems Paul was talking about is others, who normally would marry, should not (if they can "control" their sexual desires; cf. v. 9), in order to avoid the dire consequences that come to families during such periods. But those who are single (v. 8) may marry if their sexual desires are too strong for restraint. It is "better to marry than to burn" (v. 9). How important to give a good judgment as you see it to counselees, but always "to concede" what the Scriptures themselves concede, about marriage or any other issue.

Paul now turns to those who are married (v. 10a). In contrast to the good advice he has just given, Paul now makes it abundantly clear that he is no longer giving mere advice, but an authoritative "instruction" or "command" that he received from Jesus ("the Lord"; in Paul, "Lord" invariably refers to Christ). What is this? Neither Christian wives nor husbands should divorce one another (vv. 10, 11). The word "separate" (*chorizo*) used in verse 10 has confused many. The law in Paul's time knew no such thing as a legal "separation." And, indeed, Paul had spoken strongly against any separation (legal or otherwise) in verse 5. Any counselor who advises separation is advising his counselee to sin, to violate the injunction found in verse 5. This is seriously poor counsel!

Well, to what does the "separation" in verses 10 and 11 refer? Separation *by divorce*. We know this not only because the Greek word *chorizo* is one of several words frequently used to mean "divorce," but because (according to v. 11) the separation produces an "unmarried" (*agamos*)

47

12 To the rest I (not the Lord) say: If any brother has an unbelieving wife and she agrees to live with him, he must not divorce her.

13 And a woman who has an unbelieving husband who agrees to live with her must not divorce him.

14 The unbelieving husband is sanctified by his wife and the unbelieving wife is sanctified by the husband. Otherwise your children would be unclean, but now they are holy.

---

state. It is unquestionably certain, then, that the "separation" referred to in verses 10 and 11 is separation *by divorce.*[1]

The command of our Lord, says Paul, is that Christians who are married must *not divorce* one another (the Greek word *apheime,* "put away," used in v. 11, is another term frequently used for divorce). And notice, *this prohibition is emphatically stated as a command.* All biblical orders, instructions and commands are to be obeyed. There are no concessions here. This is *not* advice. To violate this command is to sin. This is important to remember since verse 11a is (wrongly) understood by some as a legitimate concession—that she *may* separate if she wishes.

Paul is giving no such concession. His Lord's "authoritative instruction" stands: "A wife must not separate from her husband." But Paul (ever the realist, who understands that Christians do not always obey) says, "if she does"—that is, if she sins by disobeying Christ's command—she must not marry another because that (especially when thought of in terms of Deuteronomy 24) would create a situation that is irremediable. Rather, she must "remain unmarried" (*agamos*), that is, remain in a condition where it is possible for others to counsel her to repent and remedy her sinful ways or, better still, she may regret her sin, repent on her own, and be "reconciled" to her husband (by remarriage, of course). To understand the principles in these two verses is one essential to doing proper marriage counseling.

To continue, Paul now addresses his words to Christians who are married to spouses who are not saved. He does not, thereby, *allow* believ-

---

1. All divorces, even sinful, illegitimate ones (as Deut. 24 also makes plain), break the marriage tie. Marriage obligations (and privileges) do not persist after divorce, even when one is obligated to be reconciled and remarry. Such persons are *agamos* ("unmarried"), we see here; they are NOT "still married in God's sight" as some (with no Biblical support) say.

15 But if the unbeliever wants to separate, let him separate. Under those circumstances the brother or sister isn't bound; but God has called you to peace.

16 Wife, how do you know whether you will save your husband? Or you, husband, how do you know whether you will save your wife?

---

ers to marry unbelievers (v. 39b), but he does recognize that this happens. Many then, as also today, are married while still unsaved. Then a partner is converted and the unequal yoke is a reality. "To the rest" means "To those of you who are not married to a believer, let me tell you God's will for you" (even though, while on earth Jesus only spoke about divorce between two believers). The believer *must not* divorce his unbelieving partner *if* that partner "agrees to live with" him (vv. 12, 13). This is the first rule. But notice, it explicitly contains a condition—"if he agrees...." That means, of course, if the unbeliever does not agree to live with him *he may obtain a divorce*. Those who wish to impose Roman Catholic absolutism upon Bible-believing Christians choose to ignore this qualification. To deny the right of divorce when the unbelieving partner wants to separate by divorce is to ignore Paul's very plain qualification.

Paul gives a second rule: try to hold the marriage together, even though you are unequally yoked, so that the possibility of winning your partner to Christ will not be jeopardized (v. 14). The unbeliever, he says, is "sanctified" ("set apart") by the presence of the believer in the marriage. That is to say, the unbeliever is placed in an advantageous position to hear and believe the Gospel from his saved partner (cf. v. 16). And, he adds, don't divorce because of your children. The child of a believer, by virtue of baptism into the covenant community, is considered "holy" (i.e., "set aside" from children of unbelievers—v. 14). Otherwise, they must be viewed by the church as "unclean" (the word used by Jews for Gentile children outside the visible, covenant community).

Now, the 15th verse is of great importance to counselors. If the unbeliever does not "agree" to live with the believer (vv. 12, 13) but wants to "separate" (*chorizo*: again, separate by divorce), the brother or sister must not stand in his way. Rather, he must "let him separate" (a permissive imperative). Having done all to hold the marriage together, if the unbeliever still wants a divorce, the believing partner must agree to it. And, when he does, he is no longer under the bonds of marriage. God wants no loose ends; there must be reconciliation or divorce—a resolution of diffi-

17 In any case, each person should walk as the Lord has assigned him, as God has called him. This is what I am ordering in all of the churches.

18 Was one circumcised when he was called? He must not desire to be uncircumcised. Was another uncircumcised when he was called? He must not desire to be circumcised.

19 Circumcision is nothing and uncircumcision is nothing; what counts is keeping God's commandments.

20 Each person should continue in the calling that he had when he was called:

21 Were you called as a slave? Don't let that bother you (but, of course, if it becomes possible for you to go free, take advantage of the opportunity).

22 The one who was a slave when he was called by the Lord is the Lord's freedman; in the same way the one who was a free man when he was called is Christ's slave

---

culties one way or another—He has "called you to peace." *Peace* means to a final resolution of the matter. Too many counselors, meaning well but doing great harm, have advised Christian wives (for instance) whose unsaved husbands wanted out of the marriage to "just keep on praying." With no divorce, the husband, who may even leave the home, has the right to return at any time. The wife, still "bound" by marriage obligations, is required to have sexual relations. Having stayed long enough to have sex, a few good meals and his clothes washed, he may leave again, having gotten her pregnant. It is this sort of on-again-off-again uncertainty that Paul says God wants to put to an end: "God has called you to peace."

May the believing partner instigate the divorce? It would seem so. The Greek of verse 15 reads, literally, "if the unbeliever is separating," that is, if he is *in the process of* breaking up the marriage. Certainly it would refer to actions (or lack of action) on his part that would indicate he no longer wishes to be married and probably also pertains to a failure to assume the obligations of marriage. According to Exodus 21:10, minimal requirements for a marriage on a husband's part are food, clothing (or shelter) and sexual relations. When these are not provided by neglect or refusal, the marriage may be terminated by the other party. At any rate, the overarching principle is that failure on the part of a marriage partner to maintain the semblance of a home, in such a way that it is constantly upset by such failure, provides opportunity for divorce, leading to "peace" for the Christian partner.

One last observation with reference to verse 15. The permissive imperative, "let him separate," does not allow the believer to contest the

23 (you were purchased at a price; don't become slaves of human beings).
24 Brothers, let each one remain with God in that state in which he was when he was called.

25 Now, I don't have any order from the Lord about virgins, but I offer my opinion as one who has become trustworthy by the Lord's mercy.
26 Because of the impending crisis, it is my view that it is well for a person to remain in the state in which he is.
27 Are you bound to a wife? Don't seek to be released. Have you been released from a wife? Don't seek a wife.
28 But if you do marry, there is no sin in doing so. However, you will have affliction in the flesh, and I am trying to spare you.

29 What I am trying to tell you brothers is this: the time is short. From now on, let those who have wives be like those who have none.
30 those who weep like those who don't weep, those who rejoice like those who don't rejoice, those who buy like those who have nothing,
31 and those who use the world like those who abuse it. The shape of things in this world is giving way.
32 But I want you to be free from worry. The unmarried man is concerned about the Lord's affairs—
33 how he may please the Lord. But the married man is concerned about the world's affairs—how he may please his wife.

---

divorce in order to try to hold the marriage together. The believer, however reluctantly, after having done all possible to maintain the marriage, unsuccessfully, must let the unbeliever have the divorce he or she wishes.

Verses 17-24, coming on the heels of those immediately before, seem also to refer to marriage and divorce. However a person may find himself at the time of his conversion—married, single, divorced—is how he should remain if possible. During persecution is probably not a time to seek to make radical changes. Paul is speaking of marriage, but uses, *as illustration*, circumcision and slavery (vv. 18-23). The core principle is given in verse 17 and reiterated in verses 20 and 24.

With reference to fathers giving away their virgin daughters in marriage, Paul says he has no specific instruction from Christ (v. 25). But as a trustworthy apostle he gives his judgment: it is better to stay single (v. 26), "stay as you are." This point he illustrates in verse 27—if married, don't seek a divorce; if divorced, don't seek to be married. But if a divorced person does remarry, it is not a sin (v. 28a); and so too it is not a sin for a virgin to marry (v. 28b). Paul's advice is meant, he says, to spare the great physical afflictions that the coming persecution would bring upon them

34 and his concerns are divided. Also, the unmarried woman or the virgin is concerned about the Lord's affairs—that she may be holy both in body and in spirit, but the married woman is concerned about the world's affairs—how she may please her husband.

35 I say this for your benefit, not to bridle you by it, but rather to promote decency and undivided devotion to the Lord.

36 Now if anybody thinks that he is treating his virgin improperly, if she is getting to be beyond her prime, and something ought to be done, let him do what he wants, there is no sin in that—let them marry.

37 But whoever is firmly convinced in his heart, who has no necessity, and has a right to act as he wishes, and has decided in his own heart to keep his virgin unmarried, he will do well.

38 So then, both the one who opts for the marriage of his virgin does well and the one who opts against her marriage does better.

(v. 28c). It will not be long before it comes (v. 29). When it comes, it will disorder everything: normal life conditions will disappear (vv. 30, 31). Paul's concern is to free them from worry, to enable them to live as faithfully and fully under such conditions as possible (v. 32). After all, even in normal circumstances, marriage involves obligations and concerns that divert one from entire concentration on the Lord's affairs (vv. 33, 34). Think what it will be like in persecution!

All he has written from verse one on, Paul says, has had two objects: to promote decency and devotion to Christ. He has no intention of bridling (putting restrictions on) anyone (v. 35). That is why he is extremely careful to make every legitimate concession possible. Instead of using this chapter legalistically, as some do, it should be used in precisely the opposite way.

Indeed, lest he should be misunderstood, he makes one final observation about virgins and their fathers (vv. 36-38). If a father genuinely thinks ("in his heart") that he is not treating his daughter properly, he may allow her to marry. It is not sin to do so. He might do "better" to have her remain single, but if he truly thinks he is wronging her by doing so he should follow his own judgment in the matter.

While Christian fathers have no absolute right to forbid or allow daughters to marry in our culture, still their influence ought to be strong. And while at the time of writing there is no persecution that would recommend them to urge singleness, there are many situations where desperate daughters would marry *anyone* rather than remain unmarried, in which case fathers should insist that it is "better" not to marry.

39 A wife is bound to her husband for so long as he lives. But if her husband dies she is free to marry anyone that she wants to, but only in the Lord.

40 Nevertheless, in my opinion she will be happier if she remains as she is—and I also think that I have God's Spirit.

Paul makes a final note on remarriage after death: it is perfectly acceptable, so long as the wife remarries a believer (v. 39). My inspired judgment ("I have God's Spirit" in saying this), however, is that during a time of persecution she will be happier if she stays single (v. 40).

Note, throughout the chapter there is both the "good" and the "best." Some Christians fail to recognize such distinctions. But within absolute, biblical parameters, such judgment calls exist. Do you, as a counselor, recognize them?

CHAPTER 8

1 Now concerning food sacrificed to idols. We know that we have knowledge. Knowledge puffs up, but love builds up.

2   Whoever thinks that he knows something doesn't know yet as he ought to know.

3   But whoever loves God has been known by Him.

4 So then, about eating food sacrificed to idols. We know that in all the world there is no idol and there is no God except One.

5   Even though there are so-called gods both in heaven and in earth—as indeed there are many "gods" and many "lords"—

6   yet for us there is but one God, the Father, from Whom all things have come, including us who ourselves have been made for Him, and one Lord Jesus Christ, through Whom all things exist, including us who ourselves exist through Him.

Next on Paul's agenda (possibly also on the list of questions mentioned in 7:1) is the matter of "food sacrificed to idols." This matter he considers in detail in the twelve verses that follow. What is the issue? In the meat market, meats were sold at a cheaper price when they came from the temple where they had first been offered in sacrifice. These second-hand cuts of meat were being purchased by some Christians, possibly because they were poor and couldn't afford more costly products that came directly to market. The issue arose: Can Christians, who have laid aside idolatry, eat meat offered to idols? Was to do so, in some way or other, to participate in idolatry—the worship of idols?

Paul opens the discussion with a word to those who said "no." Together with them, he acknowledges that there is certain "knowledge" about the matter. We know, Paul indicates, an idol is nothing and to eat of meat sacrificed to idols is not, *per se*, idolatry. But to push this "knowledge" off on others who are not clear about the matter can become a form of asserted superiority and pride (vv. 1, 2). One can think he knows everything he needs to know about the issue but may be missing a critical factor or two (v. 2). The key thing isn't to know, so much, but to be known—by God (that is, approved by Him because he shows love, v. 3).

"So then," says Paul, getting down to business (v. 4a). The fact is, idols are not gods; there is only *one* God. That is the fundamental truth

7 But everybody doesn't know this. There are some who, out of habit formed in idolatry, still eat food as if it were offered to an idol, and because their conscience is weak, they are defiled.

8 But food won't bring us before God. We are no worse if we don't eat and we are no better if we eat.

9 But watch out that this right of yours doesn't become a stumbling block to weak persons.

---

about idolatry; it is stupidity. The world boasts its "Gods and Lords," it is true, but Christians know that the Creator-God, who is both Father and Son, is the only God who exists (vv. 5, 6).

All, however, don't now realize idols are nothing (v. 7a). When they eat food that has been offered to idols, they still associate that offering with the false, so-called "god" to whom it was offered and, thereby, defile themselves by actually becoming, in some way, involved in sacrifice to a false god. Thereby, they sin. This is because their consciences have not yet been properly informed: "everybody doesn't know this" (v. 7). There is, N.B., no "false guilt" here. Their guilt is real—"they are defiled." When anyone violates his conscience (that is, does what he believes is wrong) he sins, even if the act in itself is not sinful. If he thinks something is a sin against God (in this case, to eat the meat) even if it isn't, for *him* to do it, is sin. Why? Because his attitude toward God was wrong. If he went ahead and did what he thought was (or even might be) an offense against God, he was *willing* to offend God. That *attitude* is sin.

Food, eaten or not, Paul says, is not the point (v. 8). The point, in addition to the matter of conscience, is one's attitude toward his brother. Certainly you have the "right" to eat, but your "rights" are always limited by their effect on others (v. 9). This principle every counselor must understand. The principle in verse 9 is larger than the occasion to which it applies and is very useful in counseling, especially where a counselee is demanding his "rights." We have already seen it at work in chapter six in relation to quarreling and inconsiderate Christians in Corinth; you will find it invaluable in many counseling situations.

But let us be clear. Paul is not saying a Christian should not do something that "offends" another, as some misread him; what he is saying is that if one's example causes a weak brother "to offend" (lit., "to stumble"; i.e., to sin) he should cease doing what he (otherwise) has a perfect right to do until such a time as the brother gains adequate knowledge about the issue (vv. 9-13). Exercising one's "rights" in ways that lead a brother, by

10   If anybody sees you—the one who has knowledge—sitting at a table in an idol's temple, may he not, with his weak conscience, be encouraged to eat food sacrificed to idols?

11   And so, this weak brother for whom Christ died is destroyed—by your knowledge!

12   By thus sinning against your brothers and wounding their weak conscience you sin against Christ.

13   Therefore, if food causes my brother to stumble, I shall never eat meat again, lest I cause my brother to stumble.

---

your example, into sin, becomes sin for the stronger brother (v. 12). He sins against his weaker brother and against Christ, Who died for him (vv. 11-12).

The emphasis on "knowledge" in several verses (vv. 1-4, 7, 10, 11) indicates that something was said in the letter to Paul about the superior "knowledge" that some had over others and how, since they "knew" eating meat was not idolatry *per se*, it was assumed all right to do so—regardless of its effect on others. Paul soundly refutes the idea, making each Christian "his brother's keeper" (guardian). He ends the discussion with a ringing declaration: "If eating this meat leads my brother into sin, I'll never eat meat again!" That is a powerful refutation of the "I have a right to do it" view of inconsiderate, unloving brethren.

CHAPTER 9

1 Am I not free; am I not an apostle? Haven't I seen Jesus our Lord? Aren't you my work in the Lord?

2   If to others I am not an apostle, certainly I am to you, since in the Lord you are the seal of my apostleship.

3 My defense to those who are investigating my claims is this:

4   Don't we have a right to eat and drink?

5   Don't we have a right to take along a sister as a wife, like the rest of the apostles, and our Lord's brothers and Cephas?

6   Or is it only Barnabas and I who don't have the right not to work?

7 Who serves as a soldier at his own expense? Who plants a vineyard and doesn't eat its fruit? Or who shepherds a flock and doesn't drink some of the milk?

8   Am I speaking from a human viewpoint, or does the law also say these things?

Paul has been discussing the forfeiting of "rights" for the sake of a brother (ch. 8). That discussion leads him naturally into the next: the challenge to his authority and apostleship. They said that, unlike other apostles and missionaries, Paul did not marry and usually took no salary from the mission churches he served. It looked to them, they said, as if Paul were not an apostle after all and that he had none of the rights appertaining thereto. How very wrong they were is the import of Paul's next dissertation.

Bursting forth in a volley of questions, he challenges their claim. Doesn't he have all the qualifications of an apostle? And all the "rights?" Paul rings the changes on the word "rights." He uses the word (*exousia*: also means "conferred authority") over and over again throughout verses 4-18 to some who were "investigating" Paul's "claims" (v. 3). He defends his willingness to forgo his apostolic and ministerial rights before them by issuing an additional challenge in the form of an even longer barrage of pointed questions (vv. 4-12). The defense, in substance, is that of course he has every right, as a minister of the Word, to avail himself of the very same privileges James and Peter do. He illustrates by the soldier, the vinekeeper and the shepherd, all of whom enjoy the fruits of their labor, how it is only logical to think he should (v. 7). But of more importance, says Paul, what does the Bible teach (v. 8)? Well, the Old Testament even for-

57

9   It is written in Moses' law, **Don't muzzle an ox when it is threshing.**
It isn't about oxen that God is concerned, is it?

10   Isn't He really speaking about us? It was written for us, because when
the plowman plows, and the thresher threshes he should do so in hope of
having a share of the crop.

11   If we have sown spiritual seed among you, is it too much to expect to
reap material benefits from you?

12   If others can share this right over you, shouldn't we even more so? But
we didn't use this right; instead we put up with all sorts of things rather
than place any obstacle in the way of the good news of Christ.

13   Don't you know that those who work with the sacred things eat food
from the temple, and those who attend to the altar share in what is sacrificed on the altar?

14   In the same way the Lord gave orders that those who announce the
good news should live by announcing the good news.

15   But I haven't made use of any of these rights. And I am not writing
this so that in this way I might realize such benefits for myself. I would
rather die than to have anyone deprive me of this reason for boasting.

---

bids muzzling the ox that treads out the grain (vv. 9, 10). While the principle that someone should live from the gains of the work he does is
imbedded in a passage regarding oxen, Paul insists that the principle is
larger than the context in which it is found, and that if it pertains to the
lesser (oxen), then surely it applies to the greater (men; and...men doing
God's work!). For good measure, he throws in two more examples—the
plowman and the thresher (v. 10)—and makes a powerful application in
verse 11: If we have worked to give you spiritual good (the greater), then
surely you should be ready to return material good (the lesser) to us! Others, who did not even bring you the Gospel message, as we did, exercise
this right among you; why shouldn't we, who did, even more so (v. 12a)?

But Paul says (v. 12b), we didn't use our rights *for your sake and for
the sake of the Gospel.* That will be his defense for the next several verses,
but, first, one more example occurs to him: priests who worked in the Old
Testament temple got a share of the sacrifices for their food. So too, the
Lord Jesus directed pastors who preach the Gospel to live from that work
(vv. 13, 14).

Now, back to Paul's suspension of rights (v. 15ff.). I do not use my
apostolic authority to insist on my rights (i.e., God-given rights). And
please understand, I am writing this way not to hint for money, but simply
to defend my apostleship (I'd rather die, he says, than lose the ability to
argue this way).

16 If I announce the good news, that gives me no reason for boasting, since a necessity to do so has been laid on me. Indeed woe to me if I don't announce the good news!

17 If I did this of my own will, I would expect pay; but if unwillingly it would have been because I was entrusted with a stewardship.

18 What then is my pay? It is this—that by announcing the good news without compensation I can make the good news known without using all of the rights that I have in the good news.

19 Although I am free of everyone, I have made myself a slave to all so that I might win as many as possible.

20 To Jews, I became like a Jew so that I might win Jews; to those who are under the law I became like one who is under law (although I myself am not under law), so that I might win those who are under law;

21 to those without law I became like one who is without law (although I am not without God's law, but within Christ's law) so that I might win those who are without law.

22 To the weak I became weak, so that I might win whose who are weak. I have become all sorts of things to all sorts of people so that in all sorts of ways I might save some.

23 I am doing all of this for the sake of the good news so that I may become a partner with others in it.

"Now don't misunderstand my words about boasting," Paul says in effect. "There is nothing to boast about in the preaching of the Gospel. God laid that ministry on me as something I *must* do. I'm only fulfilling a divinely given obligation. Indeed, I'd be in great jeopardy if I didn't fulfill this obligation (v. 16). I didn't take up preaching as a job [the way many do today]—otherwise I might take pay—no, I was entrusted with a stewardship from God. And to that I must be faithful (v. 17). As a matter of fact," Paul continues, "my pay is *to be able* to preach without pay!" (v. 18).

Paul knew that "whoever pays the fiddler" *usually* "calls the tune." He wanted to be "free" from such an obligation to men (v. 19). Yet, even though free of all *external*, derived pressures on his ministry, he imposed internal pressures of his own by which he became a "slave" to all (v. 19). In order to win Jews and Gentiles, he became "all things to all men" (v. 22). He placed himself alongside the weak, understanding their frailties and lack of knowledge (cf. ch. 8) for their sake and the sake of the Gospel (vv. 22, 23).

Now, it is important to understand clearly what Paul is saying. The message remained the same; Paul never changed it for anyone's sake. But, while he steadfastly preserved it at all costs, *for the sake of preaching it to all*, Paul was willing to inconvenience *himself. He* became whatever it took that was Biblically legitimate to win all sorts of people. Such flexibility and willingness to adapt are essential to good counseling. Counselors work with people who have problems and must adapt to them in order to change them. At times they, too, must inconvenience themselves. Many counselees are "weak." While attempting to balance God's absolute demands for change with the loving care and help of the counselor-servant who enforces it, a counselor *must* learn to be flexible, often foregoing his own rights. No better example of that balance can be found than Paul writing to the Corinthians.

Internally imposed pressures are what many counselees need. They must not do what is required ONLY BECAUSE THEY MUST ANSWER TO SOMEONE ELSE. They must learn to serve God *because* of a self-imposed drive to do so that grows out of a desire to please Him. All counseling that fails to stress this fails. People fall back into old patterns soon after external pressures are removed. So, it is not *enough* for a counselor to point the way or to "ride herd" on a counselee; he must help him to come to an appreciation of the fact that it is the Lord whom he serves. Part of counseling, then, is to help the counselee appreciate and love the Savior more fully. While a counselor cannot judge motives in his counselee, he must discuss them with him and urge him to greater faith and devotion. Loving devotion does not grow out of exhortation so much as it does holding Christ and His saving and sanctifying work ever before a counselee's eyes. But now back to Paul.

One item in particular might be noted: in verse twelve, Paul says that he "put up with all sorts of things" rather than place any obstacle in the way of preaching the Gospel. Willingness to "put up" with people (and those with whom one must "put up" come in large numbers to counselors) is of absolute necessity to good counseling.

In closing this section of the chapter, it is of the greatest importance to notice how easily financial matters may hinder one's ministry, and how far Paul goes to steer clear of every and any possibility of being accused of motives of financial gain. Counselors have not always been careful in this regard. As I write, I am thinking of a counselor, operating in a church, who I was told has charged a counselee over $40,000. There is something wrong with that! Paul makes his motives clear (vv. 15-18). Every Chris-

24 Don't you know that all of the runners in a stadium run, but only one receives the prize? Run in such a way that you will get it!

25 And everyone who competes in a contest exercises self-control in all things. They, of course, do it to receive a perishable wreath; we for an imperishable one.

26 Accordingly, I don't run like somebody without a goal; I don't box like somebody who is beating the air.

27 Rather, I beat down my body and make it a slave so that I who have preached to others may not myself become disqualified.

---

tian who counsels must be able to do the same. And the good motives he expresses, in all respects, ought to correspond exactly to his actions.

It is noteworthy that Paul goes to such lengths to make his motives known. After all, it is impossible for men to know another's motives (I Samuel 16:7) unless he reveals them. While counselees should not judge motives (that is God's task; He, alone, is the "heartknower"—Acts 1:24), counselees often attempt to judge one another's motives. It is important not only to challenge the legitimacy of doing so, but to urge others to freely divulge their true motives, as Paul does here. Simply doing so may clear up many difficulties and misunderstandings. Counselors, as well, should be willing at any time to explain why they are proceeding as they are.

Continuing in the verses that conclude the chapter (vv. 24-27), Paul reveals something more of his heart, concentrating on his goal and how he runs to win the prize: God's imperishable wreath of righteousness. Changing the figure, he says he boxes in order to win the bout, not as one who beats the air as if he had no goal. Paul wants the Corinthians to adopt the same goal (v. 24).

But, he makes clear, not everyone who wants to enter the Olympics is allowed to. Only those who exercise self-control in all aspects of their lives (v. 25a) and who are demanding of their bodies so as to bring them into subjection (make their bodies willing slaves—v. 27) will be qualified. Paul doesn't want to be all talk and no action; he wants to be in the race, not disqualified (v. 27b). And, as he says in II Timothy 2:5, he realizes he must compete "according to the rules." Otherwise he will be disqualified. That is why he subjects his body to stringent training rather than pampers it. And that is why he will not sacrifice his freedom to preach to all, under all circumstances, by not asserting his rights. It would be a tragedy if he who preached the Gospel to others would, by such an assertion, disqualify himself.

CHAPTER 10

1 I don't want you to be ignorant, brothers, about our fathers. They were all under the cloud, and all passed through the sea,
2   and all were baptized into Moses in the cloud and in the sea,
3   and all ate the same spiritual food,

Again, moving on to the next item on his agenda, Paul addresses Christian living in general, and idolatry in particular, opening the subject with a favorite phrase, "I don't want you to be ignorant, brethren." This is a negative way of saying a positive thing: "Now, let me tell you something you ought to know." In counseling, many problems arise because of biblical ignorance on the part of one or more counselees. There may have been some excuse for the Corinthians who, only then, were just receiving part of the New Testament. But now, for all but new Christians, there is little reason. Too often, it falls to the counselor to instruct Christians about basic, biblical truths they should have learned from preaching and from their own Bible study. Here Paul makes clear to the Corinthians that all he has to say could have been known from the Old Testament if they had only read and properly applied it to themselves.

The Greek word *baptizo* (English, "I baptize") does not mean "immerse," as many have been wrongly taught. It means "merse" (or "merge," as the word comes over into English through the Latin). There is another Greek word, *bapto*, used in Luke 16:24 that *does* mean "to dip" (or "immerse"). The word *baptizo*, therefore, means to *merge* or *unite* something or someone. It is used of the Spirit who unites His own to the Church of Christ. Compare I Corinthians 12:13: "We have all been baptized (united to, merged) into one body by one Spirit." Clearly, the Spirit does not put us into, then take us out of the body, as dipping would symbolize. No, he puts us into the body of Christ by regenerating us in order that we may ever be united to Him. It should be no surprise, then, to discover water baptism, which is emblematic of Spirit baptism, used as the uniting ordinance by which we are merged into the visible church. This is no place to fully discuss baptism, but at least that much must be explained in order to understand Paul's comments in the first five verses of this chapter.

4   and all drank the same spiritual drink—they drank from the same spiritual drink—they drank from the spiritual Rock that followed (and the Rock was Christ).
5   But with most of them God was displeased, and their bodies were scattered over the desert.
   6 Now these events happened as examples for us so that we might not desire evil things as they did.

Paul refers to the experience of the Israelites in the Old Testament as they left Egypt and traveled toward the promised land. His point? They all experienced the same things. They were all under the direct divine guidance of the cloud. They all experienced the miracle of passing through the sea dry-shod (v. 1). That is to say, they were all *united* with (lit., "baptized into") Moses in these events (v. 2). Together with Moses they *jointly* partook of the heavenly manna, drank from water that came out of the rock (and took strength from that greater Rock Who followed along, providing for every need [v. 4]). Yet, though *all* were *united* with Moses and *jointly* experienced those miraculous events, with *most* (the better mss. read "most," not "many") of them God was displeased. As a result, most of them never entered into the Land but died in the desert where their remains were scattered (a sign of God's great displeasure).

Many today, as in ancient times, seem to think their close association with servants of God and their joint participation with them in experiences of God's blessings will, somehow, carry them along. But mere association with or experience of such persons and things is no assurance that God's favor will fall on them. Each Christian, individually, must rightly relate to God. Attending a certain school, uniting with a particular church, becoming part of a Christian movement, just will not do it. Counselors will be forced again and again to this passage to make the point that joint participation in great events with prominent servants of God *will not suffice*.

Paul reaches back into these past events, detailed in the Old Testament, as "examples" for New Testament believers. Some think it wrong to use Old Testament incidents as examples; Paul didn't (cf. also v. 11). They may be used as examples for counseling when used properly—as Paul did. When they are used in a moralistic manner, they are used wrongly (David did "so and so," and you must too). But when God, and God in Christ, are seen as the subject of the example, that is altogether different; they are examples not only of what the Israelites did (or did not do), but examples of how God related to them. And, as Paul indicates, the

63

7   Don't become idolaters as some of them were; as it is written: **The people sat down to eat and drink and stood up to revel**.

8   We must not commit sexual sins as some of them did, and twenty-three thousand fell in a single day.

9   Neither should we test the Lord as some of them did and were destroyed by snakes.

10   Nor grumble as some of them did and were destroyed by the destroyer.

   11   Now these events happened to them as examples and were recorded as counsel for us who live at this late date in history.

---

events were recorded *for our benefit* (vv. 6, 11; see also Rom. 15:4). After all, if these events had no future ethical benefit and application to later generations, there would be little point in recording them. But, Paul says, they were "recorded as counsel [*nouthesia*] for us." The scriptures are to be read as "counsel" (lit., "our counsel"). All counselors who fail to use both Old and New Testament narration (as well as the other forms of revelation found therein) omit a rich source of material that, Paul explicitly claims, was recorded to be used for that purpose. Do not let the irresponsible overstatements of some Biblical theologians frighten you into avoiding this not-yet-fully-explored counseling territory. There are important exhortations here having to do with idolatry (v. 7), sexual sin (v. 8), tempting God (v. 9) and grumbling (v. 10). Use them to confront each, showing God's displeasure.

   But what does *modern*, swinging Corinth have to do with the ancient Israelites wandering in the desert? That might have been the question raised by members of the Corinthian church. Paul is more than prepared to answer it. The Lord knows that the human heart, subject to temptations, doesn't change with the passing of ages and the changes in the forms of temptation that come and go. That is why His Spirit saw that these events were recorded as counsel for the Corinthians (and modern Americans!) "upon whom the ends of the ages had come" (v. 11). They could not beg off from hearing God's recorded admonitions because they lived in times and places only remotely related to the ancient record.

   Now, what does the record reveal? That Israelites, having experienced so many divinely-given blessings, nevertheless, fell into idolatry and sexual sin (vv. 7-9). Moreover, in spite of God's remarkable provisions for them, they fell into such sins because they were not satisfied with what God did for them and began to grumble (v. 10). Could these same things happen today? You'd better believe it! Counselors whose counselees don't seem to think they could succumb to such temptations

12 So then, let the one who thinks that he stands watch out lest he fall.
13 No trial has taken hold of you except that which other people have experienced; but God is faithful Who will not allow you to be tried beyond what you are able to bear, but rather, will provide together with the trial the way out so that you may be able to endure it.
14 Therefore, my dear friends, flee from idolatry.

---

should be told, "...let the one who thinks that he stands watch out lest he fall" (v. 12). Everyone may, all too easily, fall under testing and trial.

Since most counselees are suffering trial or temptation in some form, the warning is timely. Under stress, many counselees grumble and complain. When dissatisfied with the providential workings of God, one often begins to look about for satisfaction elsewhere. This may readily lead to sexual sin (quick gratification) and/or one of the modern forms of idolatry (making money, fame, power, people, possessions, etc., one's god—see Col. 3:5).

But no one need fall. In a great verse (v. 13), applicable to counselees in all sorts of trials (that could lead to sin if not met biblically), Paul says that God has provided all that any Christian needs to stand rather than fall. Paul observes that: 1) No trial or temptation is unique. In listening to counselees, you'd think every one of them was faced with temptation and trial (the same word is used for both in Greek) that no one has ever experienced before. Paul denies it. Others, including our Savior, Who was tempted as we are at all points, have gone through the same trials *successfully*. In this first great fact, Paul at once offers hope and removes all excuse-making.

"Yes," says another, "others may have been tested as I am, but they were stronger; I am different. I can't go through it *successfully*, even though they did." "Wrong," says Paul. Based on God's faithfulness, Paul asserts: 2) "God will not allow you to be tested beyond that which you are able to bear." Many might deny it. But when they do, you can make the point that to do so is to deny God's faithfulness to His children. I have seen that stop them cold and make them think seriously, for the first time, about their own responsibility. Paul's claim is that while no test is unique, every trial is uniquely suited to the capacity of the Christian facing it at that time, if he does so God's way. There is another promise: 3) In His time and way, God will bring the trial (test, temptation) to an end, *in order that you may bear it*. People endure many things successfully when they know that they will not last forever. By looking toward the ultimate issue, they are able to face trouble today.

15 I am speaking to sensible people; make your own judgment about what I am saying.

16 By the cup of blessing that we bless aren't we sharing in Christ's blood? By the bread that we break aren't we sharing in Christ's body?

17 Because there is one loaf of bread, we who are many are one body, since we all have a share of the one loaf of bread.

18 Look at Israel according to the flesh: aren't those who eat the sacrifices partners because of the altar?

19 What then am I trying to say—that food sacrificed to an idol is anything, or that an idol is anything?

20 Of course not. But that which they sacrifice they offer as a sacrifice to demons and not to God. I don't want you to become partners with demons.

21 You cannot drink the cup of the Lord and the cup of demons; you cannot have a share in the table of the Lord and in the table of demons.

This verse may regularly be used with counselees of all sorts who doubt that they can "go on" or "face" problems. You will find great help in it for counseling. That is one reason I have written a booklet discussing this verse, for use with counselees, entitled *Christ and Your Problems,* that you may wish to use as a handout.

Now, what is the upshot of all of this? To show that his command to "flee idolatry" (v. 14) is feasible. The discussion of the command is developed in the rest of the chapter. Paul says, "I am speaking to reasonable persons (v. 15), so listen to the reasoning that follows." In the Lord's supper, when we drink from the same cup, we all share in proclaiming our faith in the shed blood of Christ for our sins (v. 16). And we also identify ourselves with his death by eating bread. And this makes us all one body by drawing us together in the profession of one common faith (v. 17). Also, look at the Jews who still eat the sacrifices in the temple. They, too, identify themselves with what the altar symbolizes (v. 18). Now, what do these two examples tell us? Just this, says Paul: When pagans sacrifice to idols, they identify themselves with demons, who propagate idolatry so that they may receive worship from it. Neither the food nor the idol is anything (vv. 19, 20); that Paul had made clear in our earlier discussion. The eating of the meat others offered to idols, however, is *not* the same as offering it oneself. Therefore, all participation in idolatrous services is sin. By participating, one identifies himself with idols and demons. One cannot (rightly) participate in the Lord's supper and idolatry (v. 21). Then—a warning: "Do you want to make God jealous by idolatry? Well then, remember, you aren't stronger than He."

22 Or shall we make the Lord jealous? We aren't stronger than He, are we?

23 All sorts of things are lawful, but not all things are advantageous; all sorts of things are lawful, but not all things build up.

24 Let no one seek his own advantage, but rather another's.

25 Eat whatever is sold in the meat market without raising questions about it because of conscience,

26 since **the earth is the Lord's and every last thing in it.**

27 If an unbeliever invites you to dinner, and you want to go, eat everything that he sets before you without raising questions about it because of conscience.

28 But if somebody says to you, "This was offered in sacrifice," don't eat it because of the person who brought up the issue and because of conscience

29 (I mean his conscience, not yours). But why should my freedom be determined by another's conscience?

When the question arises, counselors must be ready to distinguish between that which is legitimate in an incidental association with a false religion and the sinful participation in false religious worship.

In the rest of the chapter, Paul brings together problems connected with idolatry in terms of some practical examples. The principles which open this discussion are found in verses 23 and 24. All sorts of things are legitimate, but not all are advantageous to everyone. A question that ought often to be asked by counselors is: "But, is the course of action that you contemplate for the advantage of others?" If not, it violates Christian principles. Again, not everything lawful builds up other Christians. In adopting a course of action you may not seek only your own advantage, but, rather, the advantage of another (v. 24; cf. Philippians 2:2, 3). The way this principle works out in practice is as follows: Go ahead and eat meat sold in the market without raising any questions about whether it was first offered to idols. This is acceptable because everything is the Lord's and is therefore acceptable (vv. 25, 26). A believer doesn't have to raise issues that have not surfaced from other sources. Indeed, he may even eat at a pagan's table without raising questions (v. 27). *But,* if someone does make the point that the meat was offered to idols, don't eat it (v. 28). Why? Because he has a weak conscience about the matter (that we explained earlier) or he wouldn't have brought it up (v. 28). "But," asks Paul, "why should his conscience problem restrict my freedom to eat?" (v. 29). After all, I thanked God for it; doesn't that make eating acceptable? (v. 30). No,

30 If I share in it with thankfulness, why should I be criticized for eating that for which I gave thanks?

31 Well, whether you eat or drink or whatever you do, do everything for God's glory.

32 Don't be a cause for stumbling to Jews or to Greeks or to God's church;

33 just as I please all sorts of people in all sorts of matters, not seeking my own advantage but rather the advantage of many so that they may be saved.

---

not if exercising your freedom causes anyone to sin (v. 32, see chapter eight). Thus all one does must be to God's glory (v. 31). Paul makes it his ambition to please all sorts of persons rather than to satisfy his own desires (v. 33). So imitate me in these things as I imitate Christ (11:1— this verse belongs in Chapter 10 as its climax).

The theological basis for discipleship, which includes imitation, will be discussed at the place in the Gospel of John where it is taught. For here, one or two observations may be made. Proper imitation is commanded. It is, therefore, one item in the counselor's arsenal that must not be ignored. The counselor's own life should be imitatable, as well as the lives of others who may become models for correct biblical action. Imitation is learning which comes from watching and practicing the example of another.

This imitation of Christians by another Christian, however, must not be indiscriminate. One may imitate another *only insofar* as the one imitated is, in his actions, imitating Christ. The danger in all imitation is that one is likely to imitate wrong actions and attitudes rather than righteous ones. Counselors must warn about this possibility and be careful to specify precisely which actions or attitudes the counselee is to imitate. Much of life is learned by imitation, but imitation by drift rather than by design is almost always harmful.

CHAPTER 11

1 Be imitators of me as I am of Christ.
2 I praise you because you remember me in everything and because you hold fast to the traditions just as I have delivered them to you.

Paul has just explained his determination *not* to seek his own advantage (10:33) but the benefit of others. Now continuing (there was, of course, no chapter heading in the original), he instructs them, "be imitators of me as I am of Christ" (11:1). This is an important command, of which counselors ought always to be aware. The first learning a human being does is through imitation of his parents and siblings. That is how he learns his language, his basic life functions, etc. But as one grows, even though he learns in other ways as well, it is surprising to notice how much is, as we say, "caught, rather than taught." The truth of the matter is that demonstration is still—at any age—a powerful means of teaching.

Paul, like other biblical writers (cf. III Jn. 11), presupposes that adults continue to learn by imitation (cf. also Philip. 4:9, II Thess. 3:9, Heb. 13:9). Any counselor who fails to avail himself of this powerful tool of change will find himself ill-equipped to counsel effectively.

How does one go about structuring imitation in counseling? There are two fundamental ways to do so: the counselor himself may model behavior or he may point the counselee to someone else whose behavior he may imitate. Church-based counseling (which is the way God ordered it) clearly has the advantage over other types of counseling. When counselor and counselee have contact outside counseling sessions, the counselee can readily imitate the ways of life he sees exhibited in his counselor's life. This was true of Paul, who had ministered at Corinth where he lived before them the very things he is urging upon them. He can point out to them, and they can readily recall, facts about how he conducted himself on various occasions and in any number of situations. And that is *precisely* what he does.

That encouragement to imitate one's self, however, calls for an exemplary life-style on the part of the counselor! Plainly, to use this method of imitation demands much. But that is precisely what God calls those who minister His Word to be (Titus 2:7, I Tim. 4:12, etc.). You must be practicing what you are about to preach. True, the responsibility is awesome, but *it goes with the territory.*

The second, far less personally painful way is to designate a third party for the counselee to imitate. There are many things you may not do that a counselee needs to learn how to do well. For instance, if a woman must learn basic cooking or housekeeping skills as part of a counseling assignment, it would be better for a male counselor to enlist a Christian woman who excels in such things to provide the needed model. Again, counseling centered in church is far preferable. The pastor or elder who is counseling has a wide scope in choosing and enlisting a conveniently located model in such a case.

Is there no relief from the strong injunction to model for others what they should do? After all, no one is perfect. Yes, there is; only it is not designed as an "out" for the counselor, as if he need not be concerned for his life-style after all. The qualification in Paul's command is important—for the sake of the counselee. Lest the one imitating imitate the faults and failures of his model (none of us is without them), Paul adds "as I imitate Christ." That is to say, Paul, who recognized he was the "chief of sinners," knew that the Corinthians must distinguish between those attitudes and actions they observed in Paul that were in accord with Christ's will and His sinless life-style, and those in which Paul failed to exhibit them. Ultimately, that means the counselee must evaluate what he sees *according to the Scriptures* (cf. again I Cor. 4:6).

Why bother to imitate Paul or some other Christian then? Why not simply imitate Christ? First, because you can't avoid it. Everyone imitates someone, usually *unwittingly.* Paul is calling for a conscious choice to be made about *who* one imitates and *what*, specifically, in his life one must imitate. Since you *will* imitate, let it be thoughtfully and properly done.

Secondly, imitation is important to learn what a truth means *in actual life.* Truth applied to and integrated into life, in detail, is more useful to many than truth left in the abstract, in the form of principle. Jesus did not do many of the things believers do today (cope with TV, etc.) The basic discipleship method for teaching (to be discussed in a future volume on the Gospel of John) involves not only verbal instruction, but also demonstration as well. Good counseling then will always utilize and not fail to develop ways and means of using the powerful biblical tool called "imitation."

There are ways of modeling in counseling sessions themselves as specific, brief events. Suppose a counselee must confront another he has wronged, and, you suspect, he may do so poorly. You might say, "Pretend

3 Now I want you to know that every man's Head is Christ, and that man is a woman's head, and God is Christ's Head.

4   Every man who prays or prophesies with something on his head dishonors his head.

I am Sally. Now, say to me exactly what you will say to her when you go to seek forgiveness."

"Well," says your counselee, "it would be something like this: 'Sally, I'm sorry I called you a bitch when you pulled that dirty trick on me.'"

"No, Mary. That's not the way to do it; try again, this time not making excuses."

"Okay, here goes: 'Sally, you know when you lied about me to John? I'm sorry I yelled at you and called you a bitch.'"

"Mary, there are two things wrong with that. First, you're still making excuses for your sinful outburst, and second, you are not really asking for forgiveness—you're only apologizing. Apologizing is the world's inadequate substitute for biblical forgiveness. Here, let's pretend you are Sally and I am you. I'll show you how to do it"—and he models: "Sally, I wronged you in calling you a bitch. I sinned against God and you. I've asked God to forgive me. Now, I am asking you: Will you forgive me?"

Modeling, then, can be as simple as that. Nevertheless, as you can see, it is a powerful counseling tool when used biblically.

Moving on to verse two, Paul pauses—perhaps having reread some or all of what he had written thus far—and after having rebuked and exhorted the Corinthians, thinks it is time to include a word of legitimate praise. Notice the word "legitimate." Not only should Christian counselors be honest in the distribution of praise, but, you can be sure, counselees will readily pick up on insincerity. Paul knew what every person who works with people know: there must be a positive word sprinkled in among others, now and then, in order to enable the listener to receive and properly assimilate negative ones. Counselors, in sessions that are particularly heavy on rebuke (as Paul found necessary in writing this letter) will do well to look for opportunities to *legitimately* commend the counselee.

Paul now turns his attention to the matter of authority in marriage (vv. 3-16). The discussion is interesting because of difficulties stemming from insufficient knowledge of the customs of the day. But the main point of the passage is clear: there is a hierarchy of authority from God that must be observed. God is the Head of Christ (of course, not essentially, but only in His mediatorial position), Christ is the Head of the man, and

5   But every woman who prays or prophesies with her head uncovered dishonors her head; she is one and the same with a woman who has been shaved.

6   If a woman doesn't cover her head, let her hair be cut off too. And if it is a disgrace for a woman to have her hair cut off or shaved off, let her be covered.

7   A man should not cover his head since he exists in the image and glory of God, while the woman is the glory of man.

8   As a matter of fact, man didn't come from woman, but woman from man,

---

the man is the head of the woman. This subordination system must be understood and observed. Presumably, some were contentious about it (or Paul thought they might be) so he spent time explaining what he meant and why this was so. But in verse 16, in spite of whether people bought his argument, he seems to assert pure authority: "That's how it is in all the churches—don't expect something different at Corinth!"

Paul's argument is a two-point one. First, there is the order of creation (vv. 8, 9): man was created first, then woman. And woman was created for the man, not visa versa (Gen. 2:18). Yet, neither is independent of the other: men are born of women (v. 11) and women came from man (v. 12)—and *both* are dependent on God. While there must be order and authority in the Church, nevertheless, one must never think he or she is independent of the other. That fact cuts the heart out of much feminism today.

Then there is the argument having to do with hair. Women should wear a covering as a sign of subjection to her husband. If a man prays or prophesies with covered head, he dishonors Christ, his head (v. 4). That, presumably, is because he wears a sign that would mean subjection to his wife and thus, fails to subject himself to Christ. And if a woman fails to cover her head (a sign of subjection in that day) she dishonors her head, her husband (v. 5). It is the same as if she were a prostitute (whose head might be shaven). If she refuses to be subject to her husband and refuses to wear the veil, then she has made herself fair game for other men; she might as well shave her head and publicly advertise the fact (v. 6)! For the Christian woman to wear the sign of submission to her husband's authority is also important to angels (v. 10). How? Possibly, because angels participate in Christian worship. And to have long hair is "natural" (vv. 13-15). "Nature" can mean *the way things are without doing anything to disturb them*. If they don't deliberately determine to do otherwise, people

9   and, what is more, man wasn't created for woman's sake but woman for man's sake.

10   That is why the woman should wear the sign of authority on her head—because of the angels.

11   On the other hand, in the Lord, neither is woman without man nor man without woman;

12   just as the woman came from the man, so too the man is born through the woman, and everything is from God.

13   Judge for yourselves: is it proper for a woman to pray to God with her head uncovered?

14   Doesn't nature herself teach you that if a man has long hair it is a dishonor to him?

15   But if a woman has long hair it is a glory to her. Her hair was given to her for a covering.

16   If anybody is disposed to quarrel about this, we have no other custom, nor do God's churches.

17   But in giving these authoritative instructions I don't praise you, because when you meet together it isn't for the better but for the worse.

18   In the first place, when you meet as a church I hear that divisions exist among you, and in part I believe it,

19   because there must be factions among you so that it may appear who is approved among you.

---

naturally fall into the practice of having longer hair for women and shorter hair for men. That's why the Nazarites, who did *not* cut their hair, were unusual.

The counselor, while probably avoiding a discussion of the "angels," will want to refer to this passage along with Ephesians 5 and I Timothy 2 to assert the functional roles of men and women. If people become particularly contentious about the matter, verse 16 is also a powerful rejoinder.

While Paul has praised the church for its loyalty to him and to basic doctrine (v. 2), he must truthfully say that he can't praise them for the way they conduct their worship services (he will return to this matter in chapter 14). Not only does the polarized condition of the congregation manifest itself during meetings, there are problems about how they observe the Lord's Supper (vv. 18-20).

A brief additional comment on divisions is given (v. 19). Factions, in a world of sin, are not altogether useless. In God's providence, they often prove to be the means of determining who is to be approved and who is not. Those who leave, as John said (I John 2:19), make it clear that they were not a part of Christ's church; those who stick it out (K.J. "abide"), on

20 So then, when you meet together you don't come to eat the Lord's Supper
21 since each one goes ahead ad takes his own supper, and one is hungry and another gets drunk.
22 Don't you have houses in which to do your eating and drinking? Or do you despise God's church and wish to humiliate those who have nothing? What can I say to you? Shall I praise you? I can't praise you for this!
23 Now I received from the Lord what I also delivered to you, that the Lord Jesus on the night that He was betrayed took bread
24 and when He had given thanks broke it and said: "This is My body that is broken for you. Do this in remembrance of Me."
25 In the same way He also took the cup after they had eaten supper, saying, "This cup is the new covenant that is in My blood. Do this, as often as you drink it, in remembrance of Me."
26 As often as you eat this bread and drink the cup, you proclaim the Lord's death until He comes.

---

the other hand, are "approved." Differences also help make people alive to truth. Apart from such differences, many of the creeds that define our faith by systematizing scriptural teachings would never have been written. Counselors who often must deal with the effects of church division on families, therefore, may not only decry divisions, which usually occur because of someone's sin, but may also look on the bright side as it is indicated in verse 19.

Paul devotes the rest of the chapter (vv. 20-34) to a discussion of disorders at the Lord's Supper. Presumably, there were those who were bringing lavish meals to the *agape* feast that preceded the supper and took the place of the Passover meal at which Jesus instituted the supper, while other poorer Christians brought their cheese sandwiches. Evidently, they refused to share what they had (vv. 21, 22). Others had turned the meal into a drinking bout (v. 21). These problems were intensified by the fact that the commemoration of Christ's death soon faded into the background. Selfishness and dissipation had all but eliminated the purpose of the gathering (cf. v. 20). They partook of the bread and wine and failed to see in them the broken body and shed blood of Christ (v. 29). Thus, they were eating and drinking judgment on themselves (v. 29).

As a result, Paul found it necessary to review the occasion on which Christ instituted His supper in order to remind them of its meaning and purpose (v. 23-26), on which we need not comment here. The remainder of the discussion, however, is pertinent to Christian counseling. In it, Paul

27 So then, whoever eats the Lord's bread or drinks the Lord's cup unworthily will be held guilty of an offense against the body and blood of the Lord.

28 But let a person examine himself, and out of that let him eat the bread and drink the cup.

29 Whoever eats and drinks without discerning the body eats and drinks to his own judgment.

30 It is because of this that many of you are weak and sick and quite enough of you sleep.

31 Now if we judged ourselves carefully, we wouldn't be judged;

32 but when the Lord judges us, He disciplines us so that we shall not be condemned along with the world.

33 So then, my brothers, when you meet together to eat, wait for each other.

34 If anybody is hungry, let him eat at home, lest you meet together for judgment. I'll arrange everything else when I come.

---

not only explains why some were weak, others sick and some had died—God had judged them for such sinful behavior at the Lord's table—but also warns them about future abuse and judgment. And, in doing so, he elucidates a pattern by which God deals with man that is apropos to many counseling cases: "Now, if we carefully judged ourselves, we wouldn't be judged" (v. 30). That is why one must examine his motives and understanding and purpose in receiving the Lord's Supper (v. 28). God will have discipline. The pattern is: self-discipline makes discipline by God unnecessary. But if one refuses to discipline himself he can count on God to discipline him. Discipline is necessary, otherwise we'd be condemned along with unbelievers (v. 32).

Often counselees refuse to discipline their lives—even when offered help and the structure by which to achieve it. In such cases, this passage can provide a strong warning: "Either you take the help offered and shape up, or God may bring weakness, sickness or even death into your life!" While you certainly don't want to threaten every third counselee with this truth about how God works, nevertheless, in cases where total refusal in the light of clear teaching prevails, you will be remiss in not doing so. To fail to warn of impending danger or disaster is a serious failure in counseling that may lead to dire consequences.

CHAPTER 12

1 Now I don't want you to be ignorant, brothers, about spiritual gifts.
2 You know that when you were pagans you were led astray by idols that couldn't talk, in whatever ways you were led.
3 Therefore, I want you to understand that nobody who is speaking by God's Spirit ever says, "Jesus be cursed," and nobody can say, "Jesus is Lord," except by the Holy Spirit.

Paul now tackles the problem of the misuse of "spiritual gifts" (v. 1), a matter with which he will be concerned for three chapters! Chapters twelve and fourteen deal directly with various aspects of the problems that are associated with the practice of speaking in various tongues (the Greek word for languages). Because issues, some of which can lead to severe difficulties, encountered by counselors regarding tongues-speaking are prevalent today, it is well for counselors to have a clear understanding of the subject.

One of these problems is that today many of those who claim the power to speak in tongues, thereby, also claim special revelation. "Revelation" additional to the Bible, in the end, almost always contradicts the Bible. Such supposed revelation has been the cause of great confusion and has often resulted in Christians accepting teaching that has ruined their lives when followed. I shall not deal with the matter of miraculous gifts in detail at this place. I prefer to discuss this question in my commentaries on II Corinthians 12:12 and Ephesians 2:20. For now, it is important only to discover *what* Paul said to the Corinthians about tongues (and prophecy, which he compares and contrasts with the gift of tongues) in chapters 12-14, as his words throw light on counseling. *How* Paul confronts abuses of these divinely-given abilities is also important to us. Of course, the great hymn about love (chapter 13), that grew out of the discussion and is the powerful answer to those abuses, is broader then the tongues issue and has a life of its own. Counselors, in discussing love, find that they must, in one way or another, turn frequently to chapter 13 for its application to every sort of counseling difficulty. Here they frequently find a fertile field to traverse.

But now, back to chapter twelve. Paul wastes no time with transitions. He had discussed abuses in worship pertaining to the Lord's Supper at the conclusion of the last chapter. Now, other difficulties in their meet-

4 Now there are different kinds of gifts, but they come from the same Spirit,

5   and there are different kinds of service, but they are for the same Lord,

6   and there are different kinds of results, but the same God accomplishes everything in everyone.

---

ings, particularly involving the use of foreign languages (tongues) and disorder, must be confronted.

Paul begins the discussion by reminding the Corinthians of the idolatrous way of life from which Jesus Christ redeemed them (v. 2). They had been susceptible to falsehood, indeed, led astray by it. They must now be careful that the same thing does not happen with regard to spiritual gifts. Being "led astray" is still possible. In counseling, from time to time, you will encounter counselees who fail to recognize that fact. Reminding them of former gullibility and warning them of the fact that everything that purports to be Christian is not, is an essential function of good counseling. False doctrine (summed up in the phrase "Jesus be cursed" [v. 3]) leads not only to disruption in churches, but also in homes and in individual lives. When Paul writes to Timothy, he speaks of sound ("healthy") teaching—i.e., teaching that does good to all who teach and adhere to it. Teaching (doctrine) is *not* irrelevant to living (cf. Titus 1:1), but has *great* influence on life. One test for speaking in an extraordinary way, then, is what one says about Jesus. Of course, one may say the words "Jesus is Lord" (as He Himself made clear) in a hypocritical way. But what Paul refers to here is a *genuine* affirmation.

In verses 4-26, Paul explains that Jesus gave the early church different kinds of gifts through the laying on of his hands and focuses on the purpose for which they were given. In verses 4-6 he says that: 1) gifts differ (v. 4), 2) their purposes differ (v. 5) and 3) the results of their uses differ (v. 6). Yet the same spirit gives them all. In other words, the Holy Spirit is sovereign in the ways in which he disperses gifts.

This sovereign dispensation of gifts by the Spirit contains an important principle for counselors. God is the One Who brings about the differences among us. Therefore, we should neither complain nor boast about our abilities and accomplishments. After all, as Paul notes, anything worthwhile is accomplished by God through you (v. 6b).

And he continues by saying that all God accomplishes (i.e., all that His Holy Spirit "manifests" to us—v. 7)* is done for the advantage of the

77

7   And to each one is given the manifestation of the Spirit for the advantage of the whole.

8   To one through the Spirit is given a word of wisdom, and to another a word of knowledge by the same Spirit;

9   to a different person faith by the same Spirit, but to another gifts of healing by the one Spirit;

10   to another ability to perform miracles, but to another prophecy, and to still another ability to distinguish between spirits, to a different person the ability to speak in various kinds of languages, and to yet another the ability to interpret languages.

11   But all these things are produced by the one and the same Spirit Who distributes separately to each one as He determines.

12 As the body is one and has many members, and all the members of the body together make up one body, so too is it with Christ.

13   We were all baptized by one Spirit into one body, whether Jews or Greeks, whether slaves or free, and were all made to drink one Spirit.

14   Now, indeed, the body does not have only one member; it has many.

15   If the foot were to say, "Because I am not a hand I am not a part of the body," that wouldn't make it any less a part of the body.

16   And if the ear were to say, "Because I am not an eye I am not a part of the body," that wouldn't make it any less a part of the body.

---

whole congregation. Self-serving use of the Spirit's gifts is sinful. This note, struck here, will echo throughout most of the chapter. It is a point much to be emphasized in counseling. Christians must not become lone wolves. They are part of a pack. The members of a congregation are interdependent and should equally care for one another (v. 25b). Each part of the body (the figure Paul works out extensively in verses 12-27) is indispensable (v. 22), even those seemingly "weaker" parts. Frequently, rather than asking and receiving help from others in a congregation who could supply it, the counselee comes beaten and battered because he has tried to go it alone. One of the principal factors in counseling—and a goal of all counseling—is to *restore* a person (Gal. 6:1ff.) to his place in the body, receiving the help he needs from others and contributing what help he can offer to them.

I am not going to discuss verses 8-10 at this point beyond observing that these are all extraordinary gifts and, therefore, are "foundational" (Eph. 2:20; 3:5). The critical fact is found in verse 11. The Holy Spirit produced them in the members of the church *as He determined.*

17 If the whole body were an eye, where would the hearing be; if the whole were hearing, where would the smelling be?

18 But the fact is that God set each one of the members in the body as He wished.

19 If all were one member, there wouldn't be a body.

20 But the fact is that there are many members but only one body.

21 The eye can't say to the hand, "I don't need you," or the head to the feet, "I don't need you."

22 On the contrary, these seemingly weaker members of the body are indispensable,

23 and to the members of the body that we consider less honorable we accord greater honor, and we exert greater effort to make the ugly members attractive

24 than we do for the more beautiful ones that don't need it. But God has put our bodies together in such a way that He gave more honor to the members that lack it,

25 so that there may be no division in the body, but instead that the members should care equally for one another.

26 When one member suffers, all the members suffer with it; when a member is glorified all the members rejoice with it.

27 Now you are Christ's body and each member is a part of it.

There are not two or more churches on the earth: there is but "one body" (composed of all God's people, Jew or Greek) into which the Holy Spirit has baptized ("united") them. And they *all* partake of the *same Spirit* (v. 13; see also II Cor. 1:21, 22). Throughout verses 4-27, Paul stresses each member's need of the rest. All parts of the body—even the less honorable ones—are essential. Therefore, he says, there must be no division in the body (v. 25). There should be mutual caring (v. 25b). Counselors who rightly enlist other members of the congregation to help in the repair and restoration of one member who is suffering encourage cohesion. This is to be sought at all costs. One ought not try to do everything himself—even as a counselor. It is important to seek ways of bringing in the aid of others. After all, says Paul, all are involved already since when one suffers, all suffer with him (v. 26). Counselees must be brought to the place where they readily accept the assistance of others. Often pride, leading to embarrassment, gets in the way. Pride, in addition to whatever other problems one may have, debilitates. It keeps one from seeking guidance from others while problems only worsen in the meantime. Ultimately, when matters are so far gone that they are much more

28 God has placed in the church first apostles, secondly prophets, thirdly teachers, then miracle workers, then gifts for healing, then helpers, administrators, and those with the ability to speak different kinds of languages.
29 All aren't apostles, are they? All aren't prophets, are they? All aren't teachers, are they? All aren't miracle workers, are they?
30 All don't have gifts for healing, do they? All don't speak in different languages, do they? All don't interpret, do they?
31 So always desire the greater gifts. But now, I am going to show you a far better way.

---

difficult to deal with and when they may have become a public embarrassment to all, the counselee must seek help at last. How much better if he had done so earlier! Well, it may be too late *this* time, but you should warn him about ever foolishly waiting in the future. Cohesion among members of a body of believers grows as each willingly seeks and accepts help from others. Counselors have the task of reducing their loads of counseling by encouraging the practice of the early and regular mutual ministry of all the members.

After all, Paul observes, you have everything you need; God has gifted His church with all sorts of resource persons from apostles down (vv. 28-30). Seek the "greater gifts," he says. That doesn't mean *more important* (so as to put you in a more significant position), but those which are of greater *use* to others. As we shall see, the Corinthians were impressed by those which were more sensational, not those that are of greater use to the body (cf. 14:5).

CHAPTER 13

1 If I speak the languages of men and angels, but don't have love, I am a noisy gong or clanging cymbal.
2 If I have a gift of prophecy and understand all sorts of secrets and have all kinds of knowledge, and if I have all the faith that is necessary to move mountains but I don't have love, I am nothing.
3 If I dole out food to the needy and even give away all my possessions, and if I allow my body to be burned, but I don't have love, I have gained absolutely nothing.

Certainly, the great love hymn dominates this chapter. But remember, it is set in a context. The context, which reveals its purpose, is sketched in the last words of chapter twelve, which introduce the thirteenth: "But now I am going to show you a far better way." That better way is the loving use of gifts described in chapter thirteen.

The first three verses powerfully set forth the fact that gifts and abilities are worthless apart from the motivating force and direction of love. And included among the good works of verse three are the three gifts mentioned in verse two—all of which will not continue (v. 8). In contrast, love never fails. These three gifts when activated and regulated by God's love are useful.

Note, without love, Paul says, "I am nothing" (v. 2), and without love he says, "I have gained nothing" (v. 3). Obviously, love (which Jesus said was the sum of all Scripture and all God's commandments) is the one essential that makes all else worthwhile.

It is an interesting side note that Paul can say he is "nothing." Such an affirmation ought not sit well with those who have much to say about self-esteem. People are supposed to be "wonderful," "of infinite worth" simply because they are people. In contrast, Paul characterizes a large segment of the population as "nothing." How do we know that a large segment lacks love? Because a large segment of humanity is walking the broad road who do not possess the Holy Spirit. And, according to Romans 5:5, the love God requires is poured into one's heart only as he is baptized with the Holy Spirit. And then, because that love is the work of the Spirit of God, it gives glory to Him, not to man. Counselors who have bought into self-worth dogma must rethink their value. A good dose of verse two,

4 Love is patient, love is kind; it isn't jealous. Love doesn't boast, isn't proud,

5 doesn't act in an ugly way, isn't self-seeking, isn't easily irritated, doesn't keep records of wrongs.

6 isn't happy about injustice but happily stands on the side of truth.

7 It covers all things, believes all things, hopes all things, endures all things.

---

coupled with Galatians 6:3 should help deflate counselees (and counselors) who are puffed up with pride.

The description of love that follows (vv. 4-7) is useful *in its entirety*. How many counselees are impatient? In an era when you can have it *today*, and you want it *this hour*, there is much lack of patience. Yet change takes time—and patience. Many counselees want to quit when things don't happen according to their schedules. In fact, impatience may be one reason why they are in need of counsel. Few things that are worthwhile can be obtained easily and immediately. Most require patient waiting. Impatience can lead to great difficulties. Impatient persons, for instance, are not willing to give others adequate time and help to change. Clearly, impatience with others is, at bottom, a lack of love.

But, love is also kind. It does not do cruel things to another. It is a power that wears a velvet glove. Unkindness among counselees is rife.

Love isn't jealous. It doesn't suspect others of betraying one's self. It trusts. It learns to allow freedom to them and refuses to interpret actions in a negative way.

Love doesn't boast. Braggarts go about trying to build themselves up by putting everyone else down. There is a healthy, strong humility about those who have love; it isn't proud. Not only does love remove tendencies to blow one's own horn, but it also takes away the self-focus that would lead one to buy the horn in the first place! Love isn't proud.

Nor does love act in ugly ways. The words spoken to another, the actions done are all *kalos* (the Greek word running through various New Testament passages that means something is "fine, well-done, done with care and finesse"). There is a consideration for the other person that love engenders. It is a concern for how one treats him. Love removes all ugliness of every sort from a relationship.

Central to the rest is the truth that "love isn't self-seeking" (v. 5). It is self-centeredness that creates impatience, makes one unkind to others, brags and boasts before them and becomes ugly and unseemly. If there is a dominant theme in today's culture it is self. And all we need to do to see what this justification of self-centeredness is like is to look at what it is doing to our society. There is no *self*-love here; that is the problem—we have become a people so set on satisfying self that we care little about others or how our words and actions affect them.

Selfless people—i.e., loving people—aren't easily irritated. But just watch a self-oriented person: he's annoyed if you don't pay attention to him, he's annoyed when you do. He is irritated because you didn't read his mind and do all he'd like you to do for him. Every little thing irritates him. Why? Because, in one way or another, the focus of concern is not (as he would like it to be) constantly on him. All of these items, so far, are good descriptions of problems you find in counselees and the ways in which God expects you to help them change in order to become more loving to others (the love here described is directed toward other human beings).

Love doesn't become bitter and resentful by keeping records of wrongs (either actually written down or remembered). One of the principal faults of counselees is to continually bring up and throw another's actions into his face. Love refuses to do any such thing. It seeks reconciliation through forgiveness and understands that, once forgiven, a matter may not be used against another again.

Unlike many today who want to squeeze every penny possible out of others—justly or unjustly—love always happily sides with truth and rejoices when justice is done, even if that justice is directed toward one's self. The last thing love would think of doing is to perjure one's self in court to obtain a deep pocket insurance settlement.

But that isn't all. Whenever it is possible without obstructing justice, it "covers" everything it can. It stoutly refuses to gossip and slander. It is painful when, because it is biblically necessary to do so, love must relate someone's sinful activity to another. It rejoices whenever matters can be kept as quiet as possible.

Whenever there is a doubt, love "believes and hopes." That is to say, love always thinks the best of another and, until there is solid evidence to the contrary, gives him the benefit of the doubt. Unlike disbelieving Freudian counselors, who consider all rational explanations by counselees to be mere rationalizations, biblical counselors always believe counselees as fully as possible.

Love doesn't give up; it endures. Most counseling situations require some sort of endurance on the part of one or more persons. And it is often true that before he has finished the counselor must endure much as well!

8 Love never fails. If there are prophecies, they will be set aside; if there are languages, they will cease; if there is knowledge, it will be set aside.

9   We know in part and we prophesy in part,

10 but when that which is complete comes, that which is partial will be set aside.

11 When I was a child I spoke like a child, thought like a child, I reasoned like a child; but now that I have become a man I have set aside childish ways.

12 Now we see dimly as if looking in a bronze mirror, then face to face; now I know partially, but then I shall know fully just as I am fully known.

13 Now these three things continue: faith, hope, love; and the greatest of these is love.

Love brings about all these qualities, qualities in which many counselees are sadly deficient. In order to become the loving persons that God wants them to be, they must work on each of the items in Paul's list. Your task is rather well-defined by them.

Having said that "love never fails" (v. 8a), Paul compares and contrasts love with prophecy, knowledge and tongues (foreign languages). Paul says the ability to prophecy will be "set aside," the ability to speak in foreign languages without study will "cease," and the ability to acquire "knowledge" in special ways will be "set aside."

Something is "set aside" because it is considered useless (cf. the use of the same term in 1:28). What "ceases," on its own dribbles out to nothing. Obviously, Paul is saying that these things, unlike faith, hope and (preeminently) love, will, in one way or another, disappear (cf. v. 13). In contrast to the three things that will not last, there are three things that will. These will neither peter out nor be deliberately set aside as no longer of use.

It is interesting that the two definitely revelatory gifts (requiring direct supernatural action every time they were exercised) are said to be "set aside." That is to say, they were, at a point in time, deliberately abandoned. But the ability to speak one's thoughts in languages never learned seems to have been given to and exercised by the one who received it until he died. Thus, it died out gradually until the last person who possessed it died and it finally ceased. The picture Paul draws hardly seems to extend to the last time when Jesus returns, as many think. It seems, rather, to refer to the near future; perhaps to the next generation.

There is also a contrast between what is now "partial" and that which is to come which is "complete" (vv. 9-12). To what does Paul refer? There is no difficulty in identifying the "partial"—it is knowledge and prophecy. Of the three gifts, the specifically revelatory gifts are mentioned. The *partial* revelation given through prophecy and extraordinarily-given knowledge is contrasted with that which is "*complete*." The complete replaces the partial (v. 10). The extraordinarily-given revelation, Paul says, is like childish ways of talking and thinking by comparison to the "complete" revelation. In a second illustration, he says it is like looking in a bronze mirror at an indistinct image in contrast to seeing "face to face." This is a usual way for biblical writers to contrast things (cf. Numbers 12:6-8; Exodus 33:9-11; Deut. 18:15). To be known fully, as one will fully know, is to know all one can know of a human being *by revelation*. Biblical revelation, when completed, would reveal a doctrine of man, unregenerate and regenerate, that was as full and clear as the heavenly knowledge of those facts that are revealed.

Of what significance is this for counselors? Well, clearly we have in Scripture the completed revelation from God, all we need to know about man. "The proper study of mankind is man;" that is what the world says. The proper study of mankind is *Scripture*, Paul says. Biblical anthropology is of great importance to every counselor. One may fully understand man through God's now-completed revelation by understanding the Bible, and in no other way. I shall consider this matter in other places in depth.

NOTE: Faith, hope and love "*remain*." As Paul says in Romans 8:24, 25, people don't hope for what they "see." So, since hope "remains" when knowledge, prophecy and tongues do not, the "complete" must arrive before the return of Christ. We are *still* hoping for (expecting) that. So we *know* that the complete revelation must come *before* Christ returns; otherwise, hope would have no time in which it would remain after that which is complete appears (much the same could be said of faith and sight).

CHAPTER 14

1 Pursue love, and desire the spiritual gifts, especially that you may prophesy.
2 The one who speaks in another language doesn't speak to people but to God, since nobody understands him; he is speaking secrets by the Spirit!
3 But the one who prophesies speaks to people for their upbuilding and encouragement and comfort.

Now, let's take stock. What do we know about "gifts" from the Spirit? First, "gifts" are just that: gracious donations of the Spirit that are in no way earned or merited. Indeed, very sinful people (like the Corinthians) may abound in them. Gifts may, however, be "desired" (12:31, 14:1), but not pursued. One may be enthusiastic about or zealous for certain gifts, as the term translated "desired" indicates. Gifts are sovereignly dispensed by the Holy Spirit.

Secondly, what one *should* desire, or be enthusiastic about, is not the more spectacular gifts but the "greater" or more useful ones, those of greater use for the body, those that "edify" or build up believers (that concern is going to loom large in this chapter). In comparing and contrasting tongues and prophecy, the prophet holds a higher position (next to apostles) on Paul's list (12:28). Prophecy is commended "especially" (14:1) and definitely declared "more important" (or "useful"—the same word that earlier was translated "greater" is used) than tongues (14:5). According to verse 14:39 the prophetic gift is to be "desired."

In the final analysis, it isn't the gift *per se* that counts but *why* one should desire it and *how it is to be used.* The gift's purpose is to edify.

Again, counselors must inform their counselees that "God looks on the heart" (I Sam. 16:7). He is concerned about motives, goals and intentions, not only about outward activity and words (though those must not be neglected). From the beginning of chapter thirteen that has been Paul's emphasis.

In the paragraphs that follow, Paul compares prophecy and tongues. He finds prophecy superior to tongues as a medium for addressing God's people since it was designed for that purpose—to edify the body (cf. 14:3, 4, 5, 12, 17, 19, 26, 31)—whereas tongues were designed for use among unbelievers (cf. Acts 2). Among believers who cannot understand them tongues are, therefore, unprofitable. The uninterpreted use of tongues,

4   The one who speaks in another language builds himself up, but the one who prophesies builds the church up.

5   Now I wish all of you could speak in other languages, but I would rather have you prophesy because the one who prophesies is of greater use than the one who speaks in other languages (unless he interprets so that the church may benefit by being built up).

---

moreover, is disorderly and causes confusion rather than edification. Consequently Paul sets up certain standards not only for the use of tongues, but (since he is concerned that worship be orderly and decent) also standards for prophecy, prayer, etc. The overarching principles to be followed are two: 1) everything is to be done in a decent, orderly fashion and 2) everything in worship should edify. All that causes disorder or that has no ability to build up the saints must be eliminated.

In forty verses, Paul mounts a devastating attack against disorder in the Corinthian church. Already he had blasted divisions, toleration of gross and open sin, and abuses of the Lord's Supper. Now, taking up the misuse of tongues in services and comparing and contrasting it with the use of prophecy, he unmistakenly demonstrates what he means by love as the motivating and guiding force that must govern all else. Love drives consideration and consideration leads to order and edification; that is what he wants to say.

He does not say "pursue gifts" (not even "pursue the greater gifts"), but in verse 14:1 Paul commands "pursue love." Gifts, especially prophecy, are to be "desired."

Clearly, speaking in another language doesn't communicate. He who speaks, speaks to God; what he has to say is a secret between himself and God. People in the congregation can't understand him (v. 2). On the other hand, the person who prophesies speaks to the people and does them good (14:4; note, comparing the three purposes of prophecy with Romans 15:14, where the same purposes are set forth as the purposes of Scripture, indicates that prophecy is but an early form of revelation).

One who speaks in a foreign language may selfishly build himself up (if he can interpret), but no one else. In the eyes of others, he is but showing off. The one who prophesies, however, builds up the Church (v. 4).

There is nothing wrong with tongues; they are God-given. What is wrong is their *misuse*. "But," says Paul, "if there is a choice to be made, I'll take prophecy over tongues every time because it is more important for the church" (unless, of course, the foreign language is interpreted).

6 But now, brothers, if I come to you speaking in other languages, of what use will I be to you unless I can communicate to you by a revelation or in the form of knowledge, or as a prophecy or a teaching?

7 Even when lifeless things like pipes or harps make a sound how will anybody know what tune is piped or plucked unless there is a distinction between the notes?

8 If the trumpet gives an indistinct sound who will get ready for battle?

9 The same is true of you; if you by means of language don't speak an intelligible message, how will anybody know what you have to say? You will be talking to the air!

10 There are all sorts of speech sounds in the world, and none of them is without meaning.

11 but if I don't know the significance of the sound I shall be a foreigner to the speaker and the speaker will be a foreigner to me.

12 The same is true of you; since you are zealots for spiritual gifts, be zealous to abound in what builds up the church.

13 Therefore, the one who speaks in another language should pray for the power to fully interpret it.

14 If I pray in another language, my spirit prays but my mind is unfruitful.

15 What is the answer to the problem? I shall pray with the spirit, but I shall pray also with the mind; I shall sing with the spirit, but I shall sing also with the mind.

The communication of truth (in a way that truly communicates), in whatever form it may occur (v. 6), is what counts. Even musical instruments must be played in such a way that they communicate; you can't just make noise (vv. 7, 8)! You are only talking in the air unless what you say is an "intelligible message" (v. 9).

Various sorts of sounds are used in various speeches around the world and they all make sense to those who understand the language they support (v. 10); but if someone says, "*achtung!*" and I do not understand German, the speaker and I will be like foreigners to one another (v. 11). The same is true of you. You are zealous for spiritual gifts! Well, then, be zealous for those that build up God's people (v. 12).

If, therefore, you possess the ability to speak in foreign languages, pray for ability to interpret them (v. 13). In that way, at least, your ability to speak in tongues can become profitable to the Church. And it is of no benefit to pray in a tongue either, unless you understand what you are saying (v. 14). You should pray and sing with the mind—i.e., with under-

16   Otherwise if you bless with the spirit, how can an ungifted person say "Amen" to your thanksgiving when he doesn't know what you are saying?
17   You, of course, may have given thanks appropriately enough, but the other person is not built up.
18   I thank God that I speak in more languages than all of you,
19   but still in the church I would rather speak five words with my mind to instruct others than ten thousand words in another language.
   20   Brothers, don't think like children. In doing evil be children, but think like adults.
21   In the law it is written: "**By people with foreign languages and by the lips of foreigners I shall speak to this people, but even then they won't listen to Me**," says the Lord.
22   So then, other languages are a sign not for believers but for unbelievers, while prophecy is not for unbelievers but for believers.

---

standing (v. 15). Pray a prayer of thanksgiving in which you bless God and an "ungifted person" (one who can't understand the foreign language in which you are praying) won't be able to give assent (say "amen," which means "so be it"). You may have prayed well, but the prayer is of no benefit to others (vv. 16, 17).

I am grateful God gave me power to speak in a wider variety of foreign tongues than all of you (note, these tongues are multiple; no one supposed heavenly language is referred to), but when "in the church" (the subject of this discussion, remember), Paul says, "I'd rather speak five words I understand, and others benefit from, than ten thousand words in a foreign language (vv. 18, 19).

To act otherwise is childish. Grow up! In doing evil, okay, continue to be childlike, but in the matters at hand, think like adults! This disorderly and selfish use of tongues in worship services is childish. It is sinful for adults to act in a childish manner (v. 20). Isaiah speaks about foreign tongues (earthly languages are clearly referred to here) when discussing how God attempted to gain the attention of his rebellious people who turned out to be unbelievers, who would not listen (v. 21). As in that case, so today, foreign tongues are a sign for unbelievers; they are not to be used among the faithful people of God. The implication: "surely you don't count yourselves unbelievers, do you?" Prophecy, on the other hand, is for you, for believers (v. 22).

So, if the congregation assembles and people are speaking in all sorts of languages and people who have no gift of interpretation, or unbelievers, enter they'll think you are crazy. But if everybody is prophesying

23 If, then, when the whole church comes together everybody is speaking in other languages and ungifted persons or unbelievers enter the meeting, won't they say that you are crazy?

24 But if everybody is prophesying and some unbeliever or ungifted one enters, he will be convicted by all and judged by all,

25 the things hidden in his heart will be disclosed, and as a result falling down on his face he will worship God and declare that God is really among you.

26 Well then brothers, what is the upshot of all of this? When you meet together each of you has a hymn or a teaching or a revelation or a word in another language or an interpretation; fine, but be sure that everything builds up.

27 If somebody speaks in another language, there should be two or at most three, and they should do so in turn,

28 and somebody should give a full interpretation. But if there is nobody who can fully interpret, he should be silent in the church, and he should speak to himself and to God.

29 Two or three prophets should speak, and the other prophets should judge what is said.

30 And if something is revealed to another prophet who is sitting down, the first should stop talking.

31 You can all prophesy one by one so that all may learn and all may be encouraged.

32 And the spirits of prophets are subject to prophets—

---

when they come, they are likely to be saved when they hear and understand the gospel (v. 25). Rather than think you are crazy, they will recognize God's presence in your midst.

The upshot of all of this is that you are a disorderly crowd when you meet. People all come with various goals and try to do a variety of things all at once. It's okay to have all these things, but if not presented properly, they will not edify. This first test is "does it edify?" (v. 26).

If you *must* have people speak in foreign languages, then this is how it must be done: 1) only a few (two or three at most), 2) in turn (not at the same time or with interruptions) and 3) only when full interpretation will follow (vv. 27, 28). If no one can interpret, tongues may not be used.

And you should be orderly about prophesying also. Two or three, at most, should speak and others should evaluate the teaching to understand how it applies. If, however, the Spirit sends a revelation when another is speaking, the first should give way to the second (vv. 29, 30). In this orderly way, all can be instructed well and encouraged (cf. vv. 4 and 31).

33 God is not a God of confusion but of peace.

As in all the churches of the saints

34 the women should be silent in the churches, since they are not allowed to speak. Rather, they should be in submission, as the law says.

35 So if there is something that they want to learn, they should ask their own husbands about it at home; it is improper for a woman to speak in church.

36 Consider this—did God's Word go forth from you? Or are you the only ones that ever received it?

37 If anybody thinks he is a prophet or a person with spiritual gifts, let him know fully that what I am writing to you is the Lord's commandment.

38 But if anybody disregards this, disregard him.

39 So then, my brothers, have a desire to prophesy, and don't forbid anybody to speak in other languages.

40 But let everything be done decently and in order.

And there must be no uncontrolled prophesying. All you say can (and must) be under your control (v. 32). There is no confusion in God and He allows none in His church (v. 33). So then, let all be done in an orderly fashion.

Another matter pertaining to order in worship: women must not teach in churches (v. 34; cf. I Tim. 2:11-15). Nor should they speak out, interrupting others to ask questions. They should, rather, ask their own husbands when they get home (vv. 34, 35).

Then, a note of sarcasm: do you think there is no policy or practice common among the churches (v. 33b) so that you are a law to yourselves (v. 36)? Do you think you alone heard the gospel? Did you originate it? Well, don't tell me by some prophetic revelation or otherwise you have different directions from the Lord. Let me tell you as an Apostle, what I am writing is the Lord's commandment. You must hear and submit! (v. 37). If anyone refuses to obey Christ in this matter, he must be disregarded (possibly disciplined) (v. 38).

So, summing up, desire to prophesy, don't forbid speaking in tongues when done properly, but (according to the second great principle of worship) "let everything be done decently and in order."

In many ways, these two great principles that are rooted in the nature of God (v. 33) may be used about counseling matters as well as those that pertain directly to worship. All must edify. Actions and speech of counselees that do not edify are forbidden, and counselors must work toward teaching them how to consider others and what they can do to contribute to their spiritual growth.

Secondly, God's nature abhors confusion and disorder. The lives of many counselees are the personification of disorder. Their work, their homes, their schedule, their life patterns are all disorderly and either constitute their basic problem or contribute to it.

In these last two paragraphs I have but hinted at ways these two over-arching principles that grow out of God's essential nature may also impinge on individual Christians; the possible breadth of applications is limitless.

CHAPTER 15

1 Now I want to remind you, brothers, of the good news that I announced to you, which indeed you received, on which you stand,
2 through which also you are saved, if you hold on to the message of the good news that I announced to you (unless your faith was empty).
3 I delivered to you as of greatest importance what I also received, that Christ died for our sins, in agreement with the Scriptures,

---

What occasioned Paul's unparalleled discourse on the resurrection that appears in the fifteenth chapter of I Corinthians? It does not seem to be one of the matters referred to him by letter. Rather, the report of members of Chloe's household probably included the word of some who were denying the possibility of a bodily resurrection from the dead. These heretics (mentioned in verse 12) were probably Greeks who believed that only the spirit (or "shade") survived. They believed in immortality, but not in bodily resurrection and consequently in eternal incorruption. Yet that is precisely what Paul had taught. It was critical to a Christian's faith, as Paul points out, so much so that if it is not true not only do numerous problems arise, but one's entire faith in Christ collapses. The message of I Corinthians 15 is that the resurrection of the body is a cardinal doctrine for which Paul thought it worthwhile to take fifty-eight verses to contend.

When you read or listen to some counselors who purport to be Christians, it soon becomes apparent that there is little for which they would be willing to contend. They have become so soft, "accepting," and "non-judgmental" that nearly anything goes! That spirit is certainly not Pauline. "But you don't understand the depths of people's problems," you may reply. Oh? Well, it seems, then, that Paul didn't either. If there was ever a congregation in which people had problems—galore—it was the one at Corinth. Yet, to Paul it seems proper to discuss this essential doctrine with them. As a matter of fact, he sees their lives adversely affected by such error as it was being taught (v. 33).

It is the duty of counselors to stand for truth, always aware that unsound, unhealthy doctrine is often part of the counselee's problem. That conclusion, of course, leads to a second: the counselor must be thoroughly grounded in all areas of biblical truth. People vague or unsure about their faith have no business counseling until they gain certainty. That does not dismiss them from the duty of counseling others in trouble (Gal 6:1ff.),

4   and that He was buried, and that He was raised on the third day in agreement with the Scriptures,

5   and that He was seen by Cephas, then by the Twelve.

6   Later, He was seen by over five hundred brothers at one time, most of whom still remain alive, though some have fallen asleep.

7   Later, He was seen by James, then by all of the apostles,

8   and last of all He was seen by me, the one whose birth was an abnormality.

9   I am the least of the apostles, one who doesn't deserve to be called an apostle, because I persecuted God's church.

---

but it does *demand* of them study and hard work to learn all they can, as soon as possible, about the truths of Christianity and the Scriptural passages upon which they are based.

The first four verses of the chapter spell out the gospel as succinctly as any: "This is the good news that I announced to you..." (v. 1). And, if you trace the preaching and personal evangelism throughout the book of Acts you will discover that it was, indeed, the two great facts articulated so sharply here that were proclaimed by all N.T. preachers. They are, as the O.T. had predicted, 1) that Christ died for our sins and 2) that, having been buried, He was raised on the third day. Anything added to, or subtracted from, that message is heresy. Here the problem was the teaching of some who had come among the Corinthians who denied the possibility of a bodily resurrection; they were attempting to remove from the gospel the second crucial element.

The message, Paul says, had been received, and it was the foundation of their faith ("on [or by] which you stand"). And the gospel, as Paul spelled it out, was "of greatest importance" (v. 3). Obviously, all counseling, as everything else in Christianity, goes back to and is dependent on the truth of the gospel.

Paul sets forth the overwhelming evidence for Christ's bodily resurrection in verses 5-8. The historical foundation and the testimony of so many credible witnesses arrayed in these brief verses is unparalleled. "If you doubt the historical fact of His resurrection," says Paul, "then go ask the witnesses—most of them are still alive! And, though I am a Johnny-come-lately apostle, I too have seen Jesus. Of course I am an apostle, though I am overwhelmed by the thought of such grace given to me even though I persecuted the Church (vv. 8, 9, 10a). But since I labored harder than all the rest, that grace wasn't wasted on me."

Now Paul lists a number of serious consequences that follow if there is no possibility of a bodily resurrection. He ties these into this essential

10 But by God's grace I am what I am, and His grace to me wasn't wasted. On the contrary, I labored harder than all of them, though it wasn't I but God's grace that was with me.

11 So whether it was I or they, that is what we preach and that is what you believed.

12 Now if what is preached is that Christ has been raised from the dead, how can some of you say that there is no resurrection from the dead?

13 If there is no resurrection from the dead, then Christ hasn't been raised either.

14 But if Christ hasn't been raised, then our preaching is worthless and your faith is worthless too.

15 We also are found to be false witnesses about God, because we testified that God raised Christ Whom He did not raise if the dead aren't raised.

16 (If the dead aren't raised, Christ hasn't been raised either.)

17 If Christ hasn't been raised your faith is worthless; you are still in your sins.

18 Then too, those who sleep in Christ have perished.

19 If we have hope in Christ only for this life, then we are to be pitied above all persons.

---

second point of the gospel he and the other apostles preached (vv. 11, 12). If bodily resurrection is impossible, Christ hasn't been raised. Our message is worthless if Christ has not been raised and you believed it for nothing (v. 14). Then, if Christ wasn't raised, we must all be lying when we say He was (v. 15). Moreover, not only is your faith worthless, but you're still unforgiven—still "in your sins" (v. 17). And those who have died, believing in Christ, are gone—they are like animals who died; there is no future hope of life incorruptible. Finally, we are the most to be pitied of all persons if there is no resurrection. All the hopes and assurances for here and eternity are smashed. The greatest news has become the greatest fraud.

So Paul reasons. It is a powerful appeal to consider the facts and their implications. When was the last time you laid fact upon fact, implication upon implication, consequence upon consequence before a counselee who doubted this or some other essential truth? Doing so is often necessary and you must be prepared to.

Glorious fact—Christ *has* been raised, the first One to defeat death, an earnest of the resurrection of all true believers. Just as Adam brought death, so Christ (by his death and resurrection) brings life to all who are in Him (vv. 20-22). But it doesn't all happen at the same time. Christ rose

20 But the fact is that Christ has been raised from the dead, the First Fruits of those who are sleeping.

21 Since death came through a human being, so too the resurrection of the dead came through a human being.

22 As in Adam all die, so too, in Christ all will be made alive;

23 but each in his own order—Christ is the First Fruits, afterward will be those who are Christ's at His coming.

24 Then comes the end when He delivers the empire to His God and Father, when He puts down all rule and all authority and power.

25 He must reign until He puts all of His enemies under His feet;

26 the last enemy that will be put down is death; He has subjected everything beneath His feet.

27 But when it says, **He has subjected everything,** it is clear that this doesn't include the One Who subjected everything to Him.

28 But when everything is subjected to Him, then even the Son Himself will be subjected to the One Who subjected everything to Him, so that God may be all in all.

29 Otherwise, what will they do who got themselves baptized? Is it for the dead? If the dead aren't raised at all, why are they baptized? Is it for them?

30 And why am I in danger all of the time?

31 I die every day, brothers, I assure you by my pride in you in Christ Jesus our Lord.

---

first; His people will rise at His Coming. Then, at the "end" of this present era, He will deliver His worldwide empire to the Father as He puts an end to all that opposes it. Now He is reigning, waiting until all enemies, including death itself (the *last* enemy), will be put down and subjected to Him. In time, all will be restored to its original condition before the rebellion of Satan and Man, and God will be all-in-all. The mediatorial kingdom will come to an end (vv. 23-28).

Back to the implications of a denial of the possibility of a resurrection. That denial creates problems for those who were "baptized for the dead" (v. 29). We do not know what this practice refers to. At least thirty different interpretations have been offered; no one can say which, if any, is correct. It was a practice, however, that according to Paul's argument was, at best, useless if there is no resurrection. "And," says Paul, "if a bodily resurrection is impossible, and the message I proclaim is false, I have suffered "every day" for nothing (vv. 30, 31)! If it is all a farce, let's get all we can *now*; forget the future—there is none (v. 32)!"

32 If, humanly speaking, I fought with wild beasts at Ephesus, of what use was it to me? If the dead aren't raised, **let us eat and drink; tomorrow we die.**

33 Don't be misled; "bad companions corrupt good habits."

34 Sober up, as you should, and stop sinning! Some of you have not knowledge, but ignorance of God. I say this to your shame.

35 But somebody will ask, "How are the dead raised?" And "with what sort of body do they come?"

36 How stupid! What you sow doesn't come to life unless it dies.

37 You don't sow the body that the seed is going to become, but a bare kernel, perhaps of wheat or some other grain.

38 But God gives it the body that He wants to, and to each kind of seed its own body.

39 All flesh isn't the same kind of flesh, but there is one kind for human beings, another kind of flesh for animals, and another kind of flesh for birds, and another for fish.

Having talked about a life abandoned to pleasure, he now pauses in his argument to explain that people who deny the resurrection, as a result, often lead sinful lives. He warns against choosing such persons as "companions." Even after establishing "good habits," such companions may "corrupt them" (v. 33). This, of course, is a very important insight for counselors who should recognize that many counselees must break off associations that lead them astray. Understanding the powerful influence of evil persons is vital in counseling all persons, but especially youth, who are so impressionable. Wise counselors will couple this verse with others in Proverbs that teach the same truth, usually, in more specific ways. The warning here, being general in nature, may be usefully applied to any sort of situation in which evil influence is being exerted. The conclusion: "take this to heart; get serious and stop this sinful emulation of wicked persons. It's time you became fully aware of the facts! Why are you still so ignorant?" (v. 34). That, too, is a question often to ask!

Evidently, those who denied the possibility of a bodily resurrection leveled certain charges against the doctrine, one having to do with the question of *how* it could occur and another regarding the sort of body with which one is raised (v. 35). Paul's answer? "Your arguments are 'stupid'" (v. 36). When sowing seed the seed must first die before it becomes a plant that produces fruit. And what springs up is from the seed, but it is different from it (vv. 36-38). And take flesh: there are several sorts: for animals, humans, birds, fish (v. 39). And the heavenly bodies are not all

40 Moreover, there are heavenly bodies and earthly bodies; but the glory of the heavenly is one thing while the glory of the earthly is another.

41 The glory of the sun is of one sort, the glory of the moon is of another sort, while the glory of the stars is of a third sort; and star differs from star in glory.

42 So too is it with the resurrection from the dead. The body is sown in a state of corruption; it is raised in a state of incorruption.

43 It is sown in a state of dishonor; it is raised in a state of glory. It is sown in a state of helplessness; it is raised in a state of power.

44 It is sown a natural body; it is raised a spiritual body. If there is a natural body, there is also a spiritual body.

45 So also it is written, "**Adam,**" the first human being, "**became a living soul.**" The last Adam has become a life-giving Spirit.

46 It was not the spiritual body that was first, but the natural body; the spiritual body was afterward.

47 The first man came from the earth and was earthy; the second Man came from heaven.

48 As the earthy man was, so are those who are earthy; as the heavenly Man is, so are those who are heavenly.

49 Just as we bore the image of the earthy man, we shall also bear the image of the heavenly Man.

---

the same: some are brighter, others less so (vv. 40, 41). Now the resurrection is similar. The body that is sown in corruption, it is raised incorruptible; in dishonor, raised in honor; in helplessness, raised in power; natural, raised spiritual (spirit-empowered). It is written, "Adam became a living soul." Christ was a life-giving Spirit (vv. 42-45). There are *similarities* and *differences*. The natural is first, the spiritual second; the earthy first, the heavenly second. We shall progress to the higher just as surely as we have partaken of the lower state.

Then Paul says, God's eternal kingdom is one in which there is no corruption. That is why, in a flash of the eye, we shall be changed. The dead will be raised—incorruptible. Those who are alive at that time shall put on incorruption and all will become deathless. In other words, they will be made fit for God's kingdom *by the resurrection*.

For counselees with physical impairments these words hold great hope. Counselors must learn to bring home their full impact. The concluding words of the chapter grow out of the comments on incorruption and deathlessness—the resurrection has removed the stinger from death. The great scorpion is no longer a creature to be feared by Christ's own. Jesus

50 Now I want to tell you this, brothers, that flesh and blood cannot inherit God's empire, nor can corruption inherit incorruption.

51 Listen, I will tell you a secret: all of us won't fall asleep, but all of us will be changed

52 in an instant, in the flash of an eye, at the last trumpet. A trumpet will sound, and the dead will be raised incorruptible, and we shall be changed.

53 This corruptible body will put on incorruption, and this mortal shall put on immortality.

54 Now when this corruptible body puts on incorruption, and this mortal puts on immortality, then the saying that was written will come true: Death has been swallowed up in victory.

55 O death, where is your victory; O death, where is your sting?

56 Now the sting of death is sin, and what gives sin its power is the law.

57 But thanks be to God Who gives us the victory through our Lord Jesus Christ.

58 So then, my dear brothers, be firm, immovable, always abounding in the Lord's work, knowing that your labor for the Lord isn't worthless.

---

died for their sins. Therefore, the sting of death—facing the real Judge as a lawbreaker—should no longer trouble them. Their sins have been forgiven. In the death and resurrection of Jesus Christ we are victorious over death itself.

The conclusion? Be firm; don't allow evil teachers to take away the precious teaching of the bodily resurrection. And, secondly, a powerful exhortation to those who "have had it" with life: sweep aside all cynicism; it is worthwhile to serve Christ. Your labor for Him will be rewarded in that Day!

CHAPTER 16

1 Now, concerning the collection for the saints, you do exactly what I ordered the Galatian churches to do.

2 On the first day of every week each of you should put something aside from whatever profit he makes and store it up, so that when I come there will be no need to take up collections.

3 When I arrive, whoever you have approved, I shall send with written credentials, to carry your gift to Jerusalem.

4 And if it seems advisable for me to go too, they will go with me.

We come now to the final chapter of I Corinthians. It has been a long and (I trust) fruitful journey for you. But, we are not finished yet. This chapter is filled with data particularly useful for Christian counselors. We must consider it carefully. The opening discussion (Paul switches subjects with the single word, "now") has to do with the collection he was receiving from the Gentile churches to be used in helping poor, ostracized saints in Palestine. Several points emerge from this brief (vv. 1-4) yet interesting passage. Note how Paul makes it clear that he expects nothing more from the Corinthians than from the Galatian churches (v. 1). Fairness was a point belabored by the apostle. Then, he advises, "each week, as you meet, bring your weekly offering for this purpose so that it will be ready when I come" (v. 2). Paul didn't want to get involved in begging for gifts when he arrived. And, perhaps of greatest importance, he anticipates possible problems about the transmission of funds and takes care to avoid them.

First, he wanted them to appoint some persons (note the plural in v. 4) of whom they approved to take the gift to Jerusalem. Secondly, he would be careful to send written credentials along with them to certify their position in the church at Corinth and in relationship to himself; and lastly, if it seemed necessary, he too would go along to accompany them. Unlike many today, Paul avoided every possible sort of scandal concerning money.

The fact that stands out here is Paul's meticulous care about anticipating possible difficulties. A wise counselor looks ahead, "sees" potential problems, and takes measures to avoid them. This may be done by warning the counselee so that he will be prepared to meet difficulties, should they arise, and/or by taking steps (as Paul did) to assure all con-

5 I shall come to you after I pass through Macedonia, because I will be going through Macedonia.

6   It is possible that I shall stay with you for awhile, or even spend the winter, so that you can make provision to send me out from there to wherever I may go.

7   I don't want to see you now just in passing, because I expect to stay with you for some time, if the Lord permits.

8   So, I'll stay in Ephesus until Pentecost,

9   since a wide door for effective work has opened to me, and there are many who oppose.

---

cerned that any difficulty will be handled properly should it arise. No one could accuse Paul of dipping his hand into the Corinthian collection if it was carried to Palestine by trusted persons whom they themselves chose to guard and deliver it. On the other hand, Paul wanted them to be clearly designated as such to the members of the churches at Jerusalem so that there would be no questions about who they were and why they were there. There had been some tensions between the Jerusalem churches and the Gentile churches. Paul was careful to avoid creating any new ones.

Then he discloses his travel plans (vv. 5-9) so that they would know his intentions and would be prepared for his visit (v. 6). This was common courtesy, to say nothing of Christian love. He did not want them to come up short should he arrive on a surprise visit. And he indicates the visit he anticipates will be a fairly long one (vv. 6, 7). Yet he carefully conditions his plans upon the Lord's permission (v. 7b). He wanted no one to think that he believed *he* was in control of his future, and if the Lord had different plans, he did not want them to think he had changed his plans for some fickle reason. All the qualifications "it is possible," "or even...," "I expect," "if the Lord permits" (vv. 6, 7) show great care on Paul's part not to be misunderstood.

We won't speak of counselors at this point, though many need to exercise much greater care in such matters, but simply suggest that many of the conflicts in Christian relationships come from a failure to qualify statements that, as a result, are taken by others as if they are chiseled in stone. "But, you promised..." you will hear one say. The reply: "Sure, that's what I wanted to do but..." Counselees must be taught to take more care in expressing plans or intentions. As Paul here gives evidence, it is necessary, in all planning, to make it clear that your plans and purposes are *always subject to God's providential working of circumstances:* "if the

10 Now, when Timothy comes, see to it that he has no reason to be afraid when he is with you, since he is doing the Lord's work just as I am.
11 Don't let anybody make light of him, but provide what he needs to send him ahead in peace, so that he may come to me; I am expecting him with the brothers.

Lord permits." Far fewer arguments, conflicts and disappointments will occur when counselees learn to carefully qualify stated intentions.

For now, Paul says, he plans to stay in Ephesus because a wide door for effective work has opened up. But, N.B., he continues "and there are many who oppose" (v. 9). The two go together. Counselees complain, "But so many things were going so well. I was serving Christ better than ever before, I was really beginning to live as He wants me, overcoming some very difficult problems, and then—THIS! Why would the Lord let this happen just when everything looked so good?" Paul might have asked the same, but he didn't. He knew that all who live godly lives "will suffer persecution" sooner or later. Counselees must come to understand that to live as Christ desires means to live in ways that are counter to the world around and that expose the sin of others by contrast. They love darkness rather than light. That is why they tried to extinguish the Light, Jesus Christ. As believers become "the light of the world," some will follow, but most will "oppose."

Paul's concern for his young coworker Timothy appears here, as elsewhere. Timothy must have been sensitive and fearful. So he urges the Corinthians—who, from indications in this letter and the next, could deal out rough treatment—to take it easy on Timothy. He is, Paul says, doing the Lord's work too. Evidently, Timothy had much to offer, but people tended to "make light of him" because of his timidity. They are to receive him (perhaps as he brought this letter), hear him, then provide for his trip (along with others) to meet Paul.

Not everyone is alike. Counselees must recognize this. While some love the rough-and-tumble of conflict, others back off. Neither necessarily is wrong. Counselees often wonder "why can't my wife [child] be like me?" Some people *must* be handled gently though that fact may easily be forgotten. Here is one place for counselors to turn to make the point.

Once beginning to call the roll of those somehow related to the Corinthian Church, Paul continues to tick them off. Next, Apollos. Probably because of the divisions revolving around Apollos and himself, Paul

12 Now concerning brother Apollos, I strongly urged him to come to you with the brothers, but he definitely didn't want to come now. Instead, he will come when he gets an opportunity to do so.

13 Stay alert, stand firm in the faith, be courageous, be strong.

14 Do everything in love.

15 Now brothers, I urge you—you know that the household of Stephanas was the first fruits of Achaia, and that they have devoted themselves to serving the saints—

16 submit to such persons and to all my co-workers and co-laborers.

---

strongly urged him to go to Corinth as one of the delegation of which Timothy was a part. But, for whatever reason, Apollos did not wish to go at the present time. But he does plan to do so in the future when the opportunity arises. To be able to speak about Apollos in this fashion at least shows that he and Paul were not at odds.

Now five commands: "stay alert." This means, literally, "stay awake." While one may not doze physically, he may easily be too relaxed about sin and its many temptations. The true Christian life is the life of the soldier on the field who, to survive, must "stay alert." Good counsel for many who, thinking they will never fall, fail to heed it. "Stand firm in the faith." There are many out there who want to water it down, add to it or, in some other way, shake Christians from a firm stand for the truth. Remaining "alert" to these forces, one will be able to brace himself for attacks when they come. "Be courageous." Paul's words all speak of conflict, battles and warfare. In battle, courage is essential. One must not run. Rather, he must "be strong." There is much to do and to endure. Strength is needed for the battle. Being firm in the faith and courageously testifying to Jesus Christ, one builds up the spiritual strength needed to withstand the enemy. Yet one word of caution (v. 14): all must be done "in love." Soldiers and warfare conjure up ideas of roughness, inflicting pain and even death—not ideas of love. While Christians must exert strength, powerfully defeating sin, they must, nevertheless, "overcome evil with good" (Romans 12:21). The "good" in view is loving acts of kindness toward enemies. The caution here is vital. In counseling, counselors often must act as generals sending counselees back to the trenches. The orders for battle they give must "all" be tempered by urging that they be carried out in love for God and others.

The household of Stephanas consisted of older, mature Christians who have served the church well. Therefore, they are to be obeyed. Paul always encouraged submission, not only to apostles, but to all who

17 I am happy about the arrival of Stephanas and Fortunatus and Achaicus, because they have supplied what I lacked from you,

18 since they refreshed my spirit as well as yours. You must recognize people like them.

19 The churches of Asia greet you. Aquila and Priscilla, along with the church in their house, greet you.

20 All the brothers greet you. Greet one another with a holy kiss.

21 This greeting I, Paul, write with my own hand.

22 If anyone doesn't love the Lord, let him be cursed. Our Lord is coming!

23 May help from the Lord Jesus be with you.

24 My love to all of you in Christ Jesus.

---

worked with them (v. 16). Evidently Stephanas, Fortunatus and Achaicus brought the Corinthian letter to Paul (v. 17) and were now returning with his reply. They had been most helpful to Paul while with him. He had directed them about the problems and sent his letter to accompany them on the return. The church must "recognize" (i.e., pay attention to) them and what they say. Counselors must counsel with Christ's authority under the aegis of the Church. Paul, also, was careful to maintain good relations between the churches of Christ. His letters, in which he conveys greetings from church to church, are evidence of this. Too frequently, today, people set church over against church. Counselors may be tempted to fall into this trap. But instead, they must follow Paul.

Paul authenticates the letter, dictated through a secretary, by signing it in his own handwriting.

At the conclusion is both a malediction (v. 22) and a benediction (v. 23). Maranatha = "our Lord is coming"; anathema = "curses on him." Two sound-alike words conveying two opposite wishes, the latter reminiscent of Malachi 4, the concluding verse.

To warn counselees in strong terms like "let him be cursed" is also a part of the counselor's task, unpleasant though it may be. You must be prepared to pronounce it on those who will not hear and doggedly persist in destroying the work of Jesus Christ.

Conclusion

This first in a series of commentaries for Christian Counselors sets the tone for those that follow. I am open to suggestions, however, of ways in which they may be improved. There is, of course, much I have not said, but I hope those facts and suggested guidelines that are included will be useful for those who use this commentary.

While I Corinthians sets forth much that one may use in counseling, it is neither exhaustive nor definitive concerning many items to which it does refer. As a result, my goal is to consult and consider the teachings and counseling implications for the *whole* counsel of God by commenting first on the entire New Testament, then (if God wills) on Psalms and Proverbs, and ultimately on the whole Old Testament. I am not so unrealistic as to suppose that I shall be able to fully realize these objectives during the remainder of my lifetime, but I shall continue until God calls a halt and trust others will complete what is left undone.

Jay E. Adams
Simpsonville, SC
1994

Introduction to
II Corinthians

I Corinthians is known for its great chapters; II Corinthians for its powerful paragraphs and memorable verses. It is, as the name indicates, a sequel to the first book of that name. In my studied opinion it is a unified document, not the compilation of two or more. It is, arguably, Paul's most personal book. Forced by attacks not only upon his doctrine, but principally on his person and integrity, Paul finds it necessary to talk about himself—especially in relationship to his ministry—even though it was distasteful for him to do so. But providentially, as the result, we learn a great deal about him, especially about his attitudes, his motivation, his purposes and methods, that otherwise would not be available to us. In the work of counseling one cannot avoid many of the problems with which this book is concerned. From that perspective, because the book focuses on the worker and his ministry, the counselor can learn much. But that does not mean that there are not also data about principles of life that counselors must understand, teach and inculcate. Indeed, the book is full of nuggets, some of which do not arise in other books or are not so fully discussed elsewhere as they are in II Corinthians. It is, therefore, an extremely valuable book for counselors.

As you progress throughout the volume, keep three things before you: counseling principles, practices and materials. If you look for help in each of these areas you will benefit more than if you overlook one or two of them. There is so much in II Corinthians that could be discussed that does not directly (or even indirectly) bear on counseling that I would like to write about, but I must forbear doing so. Using good exegetical commentaries along with this supplemental material would be helpful in obtaining a fuller understanding of Paul's letter.

CHAPTER 1

1 Paul, an apostle of Christ Jesus by God's will, and our brother Timothy to God's church that is in Corinth, with all the saints who are in the whole of Achaia.

2 May help and peace from God our Father and from the Lord Jesus Christ be yours.

3 Blessed be the God and Father of our Lord Jesus Christ, the Father of compassion and God of all help,

---

Paul introduces this epistle in a manner similar to his others. There is a word of greeting, a benediction and a blessing which, in this case, smoothly merges into the matter of the letter itself. All of this he accomplishes in three brief verses. He identifies himself, gives his divine warrant for the ministry he is about to exercise in the letter (**he is an apostle**), and mentions the source of his mission (**by God's will**). He also includes Timothy in the salutation and calls the church at Corinth "God's church." There are many who had heard about the work at Corinth, so he also includes **all the saints who are in the whole of Achaia.** It is not merely because of their interest and concern about the Corinthian church that Paul mentions the saints in Achaia. He also wants the Corinthians to know that the things he is about to discuss are of interest to others. While much has been accomplished since the first epistle was sent, there are still problems, and Achaians will be concerned about the outcome that will issue from the present letter. Moreover, later on he will want to compare and contrast the work at Corinth with that in Achaia. And since there were people who doubted the validity of Paul's ministry agitating among the members of the Corinthian church, he wanted them to know that the **whole** church of Achaia stood with him. What Paul sets up in the introduction (often, as here in the salutation itself), then, is not mere pleasantry; it is planned, purposeful material that will be used later on in the letter.

Counselors should learn from that. Things they say in early sessions—especially the first—if properly gauged, may be of great benefit later on. For instance, "Now let me make it clear that there will be no fighting, cutting words or nastiness allowed in these sessions." Or, "Contrary to some counselors, who encourage talking negatively behind another's back, I have asked you both to be present from the outset. In that

109

way, you both will know what each knows, and that each knows it. More-over, you will be able to amplify or correct statements made by one another." Those sorts of comments, of course, are rather out in the open. More subtle ones (like those we encounter in Paul's letter) also may be made. For instance, because you intend to give ample homework later on in the session, you might prepare your counselees for this at the beginning of the first session by mentioning that you "plan to work only for a limited number of sessions," and that you "want to move rapidly so that they will suffer no longer than necessary." If they give assent to this, later, at the end of the session, when they protest that the homework seems to be more than they can accomplish during the succeeding week, you may remind them that you promised to move quickly, that they agreed they wanted to, and that "rapid progress will require steady, faithful, hard work for a few weeks." Dozens of other slight comments at the outset that you may open up later may be planted as seed early on. That is the method of the apostle.

Help and peace was a frequently-used benediction because all the churches need precisely those two things. Benedictions—which express the wish that God will do good things for those upon whom such benedictions are pronounced—are tools not out of the reach of counselors as well. How often do you express such things at the beginning or the end of a session? Think about it and see if you can't come up with an expression of what you wish God to do for them, and for which you are praying. Benedictions encourage. They also identify goals. And they remind the listener both of God's ability and the possibility of God's blessing. Think about this. Can you hear yourself saying something like this: "Sam and Hilda, you have made good progress today. May God bless that hard work to bring about some significant changes in your relationship this week"?

It is not only encouraging to think about what God might do and the capacity He has to do it, but even more so to understand what He *has* done for others and, interestingly, in what follows, that which He has done for others *so that they, in turn, might help others.* Paul speaks of God not only as the Father of Jesus, but characterizes Him as the God of **compassion and all comfort**. Again, what the Corinthians (and your counselees) need is exactly what God is. Because I have developed it more fully in my book *The Theology of Counseling*, I will not do so here; but it is important to realize that every attribute of God (often expressed in one or more of His names) has vital implications for counseling.

What God is called in Scripture is not only indicative of what He is like, but also of what He does. Contrary to all humanistic counseling, and much that purports to be biblical, it is not the compassion or comfort of the counselor that is of such great importance (though you must learn to be compassionate and comforting so that those to whom you minister may not be misled about the God you represent and Whose Word you are ministering).

What really matters is that God is **compassionate and He is the Source of all comfort.** Even Christian counselors often fail to make this point to counselees. Paul made no such mistake. He was well aware that, ultimately, what he wrote and did depended not on himself (though he knew that God held him responsible to do all things well), but on God. It was to the unfailing compassion and comfort of God, then, that Paul pointed his counselees.

When counselees complain about their lot, you must show them that it is with God they must reckon. He is the exclusive and adequate Source of all comfort. It is important to understand this for at least two reasons. First, you must not allow counselees to blame others for their failures, and secondly, you must point them to nothing less than the real Source of help. Therefore it is important for them to know what God is like and that He considers it not only proper to rescue His own from trouble but, while in it, to sustain them with His comfort, counsel and other sorts of assistance (the word *paraklesis* used here has all those meanings, and more). And of particular importance to a harassed counselee is the fact that God is a God of compassion. That is to say, no matter what the trouble, God's compassion and comfort are present for the welfare of His own whether, at the moment, a counselee can fathom how or not. His compassion extends to deep concern for every one of His children; there is none too insignificant, too small for His providential care. Indeed, counselors must explain that the very trials Christians dread are for their blessing and benefit, that they are to view trials and tribulations themselves as compassionate circumstances. Compassion and pity were looked upon unfavorably by the Romans as weakness. It was only because Christianity was introduced into the world that this divine characteristic also came to be considered a human virtue. It is interesting to note, though here we are unable to expatiate on it, how the virtues of men are reflections of divine attributes: God is a God of compassion (the word used by Paul means, literally, a "feeling of distress for others").

Now, notice the little word "all." When God's children turn to other sources of comfort they grieve the heart of God. His comfort is adequate. There is no real comfort anywhere else; God is the God of **all** comfort. True, others may mediate it to the counselee—as the counselor who ministers God's Word does—but comfort that does not originally flow from

4   Who helps us in all of our afflictions to make us capable of helping persons in every sort of affliction by the help with which God helped us.
5   Just as we experience Christ's sufferings in abundance, so too through Christ we experience an abundance of help.
6   When we are afflicted, it is for your help and salvation; when we are helped, it is to help you so that you may effectively endure the same sufferings that we also are suffering.
7   Our hope for you is firm, since we know that as you share in our sufferings, so too you will share in our help.
8 Now we don't want you to be ignorant, brothers, about the affliction that we suffered in Asia, how we were burdened far beyond human ability, so that we even despaired of life.

His Word will be found false, unstable and an ultimate failure. Even when the counselor mediates Scriptural comfort, he must always make it clear that it is not he, but God, Who assures us of the truths he discloses. God must always be the One to whom the counselor brings the counselee, in his complaints as well as in gratitude. Never forget, ultimately it is God, not you, with Whom your counselee must deal. Make him feel that from the outset.

Counseling is a ministry of assistance to those who are afflicted and in trouble. Counselors assist and comfort by bringing the comfort and help of the Scriptures to bear on the problems of counselees. The ministry of assistance, therefore, is the ministry of the Word—nowhere else can the comfort and assistance of God be found. God uses people to minister His Word, but they who bring comfort and assistance have nothing to offer apart from that Word (cf. Romans 15:5, 4).

In verse four Paul speaks of the comfort that God has given to him and his associates, as he puts it, **in all our afflictions**. What these were we shall have occasion to notice in detail when we come to the 6th and 11th chapters of this book. Suffice it to say, they were more severe and more extensive than those experienced by anyone you will ever counsel. It is often useful when using this passage from chapter one to read those two lists in conjunction with it so that the counselee will be able to grasp what Paul was talking about. In doing so, again, be sure to note the word "all."

Counselor, have you known an extraordinary amount of affliction, sorrow, trouble? Well, that probably was because in His wise providence God was preparing you for a ministry of counseling. On the other hand, if you have not experienced the comfort and assistance of God in affliction and trouble, you may not be ready to do extensive counseling. Read the rest of the verse. Trouble comes to the counselor *so that* he may turn to the Lord to understand His compassion and experience His comfort. Having done so, he should be prepared to comfort (counsel, encourage, assist) people in any sort of trouble with the same comfort he found.

Counselees will object, "But you haven't gone through the **same** problems I have." You may point out that Paul doesn't say you must. Paul assumes that the same comfort is to be found for one problem that may be found for another. God's comfort is God's comfort. It is the comfort that is similar—regardless of how problems may differ. This is true because the principles of comfort are the same whatever the problem may be. And the One from whom comfort comes is the same. After all, recognizing the sovereignty of a caring, omnipotent and omniscient Father who is in control of the universe and working all things together for your good (for example) is, in fact, comforting in any and all situations, isn't it? So, a woman who loses a child in a miscarriage may be comforted by a woman who is unable to bear children. Both have suffered loss; both need to trust in and find comfort from the God Who does all things well. Each might comfort the other. Ministers doing hospital visitation encounter people with all sorts of physical problems. These may be quite diverse, but the basic biblical principles of handling sickness are not.

Paul was even able to say that because he experienced much affliction, this meant that he had experienced much comfort. It is not too far-fetched, also, to observe that the counselee may be experiencing much affliction to draw him closer to God through the reception of His gracious and all-sustaining comfort so that, at length, when his trials are over, he may be able to comfort others in trouble (cf. esp. vv. 4, 6). After all, when Peter was turned around, he was expected to "strengthen" his brothers. The comfort that he received from the Lord (John 21) made that possible. The counselor receives the blessings of *paraklesis* not for himself alone, but to prepare him for ministering to others who will need it.

Notice too, the comfort that Paul extends to others (v. 4) is not some self-generated comfort, but the same comfort he received from God when he was in trouble. Counselor, certainly verse 6 ought to be one to which you turn for understanding whenever you yourself fall into various afflictions. Stop complaining and seek to discover the comfort of the compassionate One who sent trouble your way to enable you to experience His comfort—so that, at length, you can comfort others. Your own suffering and comfort is part of your training.

After all, much of what your counselees need is to learn to **effectively endure the same sorts of sufferings** that you do. Endurance is

9   Rather than expect to live, we passed the sentence of death on our-selves. This happened so that we wouldn't depend upon ourselves but on God, Who raises the dead.

10   He delivered us from so great a death, and He will continue to deliver us. He is the One on Whom we have set our hope that He will yet deliver us

11   as you also cooperate by praying fervently for us, so that many persons will give thanks for us because of the favor shown us in answer to many prayers.

---

what you must counsel in most instances. God, for His own wise pur-poses, does not always extricate His own from trials at once. They must learn to endure. This word refers to the ability to hang in there when the going gets tough. We shall have something to say of this later on in the book. But for now check off this passage as one to which you may want to turn frequently in counseling, especially whenever your counselee faces affliction that it seems will continue unrelieved, for at least the immediate future.

Paul had reason to hope (v. 7), and he took the trouble to let his read-ers know so. When you are encouraged with the progress of your counsel-ees, tell them. You'll see Paul doing so throughout this letter. His hope was "firm." Why? Because since they had shared his sufferings, he knew the Corinthians would share his comfort. It was encouraging to know that they had endured much for Christ; therefore, there was hope.

We come now to verses 8-11. In them, we shall learn something of the trials into which the Lord led Paul so that he might suffer and be com-forted. The details of what Paul faced must have been known to the Corin-thians because he does not spell them out. There are many conjectures about them, but no one really knows what they were. What he *does focus on*, however, is the **severity** of the trials. This is the important element for Paul here. The Corinthians could not say "Well, our problems are more serious than yours, so your words about comfort do not apply." Don't let counselees get away with that. No, Paul's afflictions in Asia (Asia Minor)—whatever they were—were so bad that he was **burdened beyond human ability**, leading him to **despair of life**. He had even pro-nounced the sentence of death on himself. He thought he had come to the end of life.

But there is even a greater reason for mentioning the Asian trials. Paul wants to make the point that such difficulties often come for other good reasons. Here he mentions two of these reasons (one the flip side of the other). In verse 9 he asserts that his afflictions happened 1) to discourage him from depending on himself, and 2) to encourage him to depend on God. How many counselors and counselees need to learn these same two lessons! Counselors must make this point to those undergoing affliction. To do so is to offer a vital part of the divine comfort the counselee needs. He must be taught to stop focusing on the trial and to concern himself, instead, with the good results that can emerge from it. Trial should lead true Christians to abandon proud self-dependence and to lean more fully on God.

It is useful to observe God's ways in the lives of His most faithful servants. That He subjected them to serious afflictions forestalls any idea that all affliction is punishment. Many counselees come to counseling with this false orientation. Having investigated the possibility of self-inflicted problems (don't forget to do that first), show that this is not always the way things happen. Not only were Job and the blind man of John 9 afflicted for the purpose of demonstrating God's goodness to others, but here we see that sometimes affliction comes to bring us closer to God.

Look how far God went with His great apostle. Paul says that he was burdened beyond his ability to withstand the trial. He was like a weary animal that sinks beneath a load that is too great. He had no personal power or strength left. To survive, he had to find a Source of power and strength greater than his own. He despaired of life. He could see no way out. He was perplexed, did not know which way to turn—except to God. He was like a man on death row—prepared to die. When he put the question to himself, "Will I live?" The answer was "no." No wonder that his rescue by God was like a resurrection from the dead (v. 9)! Because of this remarkable deliverance from the very jaws of death, Paul had **hope** for the future. God would deliver him yet again.

Past deliverances from difficulty and despair experienced by your counselee ought similarly to raise his hopes during present trials. In that sense, just as in Paul's case, the comfort he received from God in the past carried him through trial and helped him to become more God-dependent. That, along with the counselor's experience of comfort, should enable him to have a twofold witness to the compassion and goodness of God.

Paul attributed his deliverance by God to the Corinthians' prayers. He and his teams (one of which seems to have been involved in these trials) did not try to go it alone. They constantly requested the prayers of the churches (cf. Philip.1:19; Col. 3:4ff.). If counselors do not have other

12 Now the testimony of our conscience is our reason for boasting, because we have behaved with holiness and godly sincerity in the world (and more especially toward you), not with fleshly wisdom, but rather by God's help.
13 We are writing nothing to you but exactly what you read and understand it to be. I hope that you will understand to the end
14 (as you have understood us in part, so that you can make us your boast, as you are ours, on the Day of our Lord Jesus.)

Christians praying for them, they are in a precarious position. There is no one who can rightly minister alone. Everyone who serves Christ needs his church—and at times other churches as well—praying for him. The self-sufficient counselor, who thinks prayer by others is but a luxury, will never become an apostle Paul.

Apparently some had accused Paul of insincerity and vacillation. They had judged him on the basis of his actions without first asking for his explanation (a common fault of counselees and even counselors). If they had inquired of Paul rather than coming to a decision from insufficient evidence, they never could have reached the conclusions they did. Evidence (as we shall see in II Cor. 13:1) is essential before making judgments about others. Counselors, in every sort of context, must remember this all-important fact.

These troublemakers accused Paul of saying one thing and doing another. As an example, they referred to his failure to keep a promise to visit Corinth. In strong terms and a quite definitive manner Paul refutes the charge of duplicity. First he says, "I have always been absolutely clear about what I write. You won't find either hidden meanings or vagueness in the things I say (v. 13). What you see is what you get. I don't write in such ambiguous language that you could take my words in more than one way—as though I said yes and no at the same time. My conscience is clear about this matter. By God's help [the second meaning of 'grace'] I have been sincere and holy in all my dealings with you. So then, what of the charge?

"Well, let me point out a few things for you. And what I am saying is true especially in my relationship to *you* (v. 12). I did not act out of fleshly wisdom—remember, I explained the difference between the wisdom of man and God before (I Cor. 2). And in part, at least, you have understood what I wrote (v. 14). I hope in time that you will understand a great deal more (v. 13). Then, when Christ returns, you can boast about your relationship toward us just as we can about ours toward you (v. 14)."

15 Because I was persuaded of this I had planned at first to come to you so that you might have a double favor,

16 passing through your community as I went to Macedonia, and then coming to you again as I left Macedonia, and from there to be sent with full provisions by you to Judea.

17 Since this is what I planned, did I proceed lightly; or do I make plans in keeping with the flesh, so that at the same time I say "yes, yes" and "no, no"?

You can see from Paul's words that his concern about relationships was not mainly horizontal. He wanted to maintain right relationships to others because he cared about the impact of this upon his ministry for the Lord Jesus Christ. If he was undependable, it might lead others to think His Lord was also. That might unsettle their relationship to Christ. That could not be. Paul defends himself, therefore, not out of any personal concern but for pastoral reasons.

He says, "Let me tell you what really happened. I *did* plan to visit you. In fact I hoped to make two visits—one on the way to Macedonia and one on the way to Judea (vv. 15, 16). What happened? Why didn't these plans materialize? Because I am not dependable and make promises I don't keep? No. My promises are as genuine as God's. Just as Jesus says 'yes' and doesn't mean 'no,' so too you can depend on my word. When I say 'yes' I mean yes. Christ doesn't vacillate; neither do we (here he mentions the names of the other members of his team at last—v. 19). Why then didn't I come? Because I am weak? No, God made us firm by uniting us to Christ Who is firm, and by anointing me with His enabling Spirit. I refer to the indwelling Spirit Who is the downpayment on our eternal inheritance.

"The reason I didn't come was because I deliberately changed my plans. And I ask God to bear me witness (putting my soul on trial before Him) that I did so FOR YOUR SAKE. I determined to spare you. I wanted to come, but not with a rod, not in the embarrassment that would have meant for all of us. So I decided to give you time to get your house in order. I did this only because I knew you were fundamentally firm in your faith. And I didn't want to lord it over you, but wanted you—on your own—to make the necessary changes I had enjoined in my letter."

Of what benefit is all of this to you, counselor? For one thing, it should teach you not to vacillate. Don't make promises you don't intend to keep—or can't keep. Let your yes be yes. Keep a clean conscience about such things. Secondly, at times changes may be necessary. And it is

18 But as surely as God is dependable, our word to you has not been yes and no.
19 After all, God's Son, Christ Jesus, Whom we preached to you (Silvanus, and Timothy and I), wasn't yes and no; rather it has always been yes in Him.
20 All God's promises are yes in Him. Indeed, that is why we say our "Amen" through Him to God's glory.

---

not always wrong to change your plans. But when you do, always explain fully your motives in making changes. Otherwise counselees may misunderstand. Lastly, learn that there is a time to back off, a time not to confront, a time when you should wait to see what the counselee himself will do. You cannot do everything for him. You dare not lord your stronger personality or authority over him. Otherwise he will become dependent on you. There is a time (given his basic firmness in the faith) to see how he will respond to your previous exhortations. After all, the Spirit is at work within him.

How do you know when to confront and when not to? Of course, a judgment must be made, and cases differ. You cannot read another's heart. But when you see a basic firmness of faith, when you recognize that a counselee understands enough to make the changes required (v. 13), all other things being equal, that may indicate it is time to back off. You don't always want to be scolding the counselee like an irritable father scolding his son! It is well, whenever possible, to avoid such confrontations. Fundamentally, you can say the time to "spare" is when there seems to be a willingness to change and there is good reason to think your counselee might make such changes on his own. Paul took a *calculated* risk. The Corinthians' faith was OK; it was their conduct that needed improvement.

Verse 24 is interesting. The counselor is not an expert or a magician who "does it for and instead of" his counselees in some magic hour. He does not make counselees dependent on him and his expert, esoteric knowledge. He teaches the counselee all he knows that is pertinent to his situation. He cooperates with the counselee, helping HIM to make the changes necessary to please God. Counseling is always a joint effort—and it does involve effort. So the proper stance is cooperation, not domination. Paul speaks of them as *sunergoi*, a term that means co-workers. The counselor, therefore, is not over but alongside his counselee as they work on problems. In not coming with a rod, that is what Paul meant to express. Of course when there is refusal to obey God the rod may become

21 But the One Who makes us firm along with you by uniting us to Christ, and has anointed us, is God,

22 Who also has sealed us and given us the Spirit in our hearts as down payment.

23 So, putting my soul on trial, I call on God to testify that because I wanted to spare you, I didn't come again to Corinth.

24 It isn't that we want to lord it over your faith (because you are standing firm by faith), but that we are working with you for your joy.

---

necessary; church discipline (as we learned in I Corinthians) is sometimes essential to the well-being of the Church. But while Paul possessed authority, he did not always exercise it. He is not here denying the apostolic authority he possessed, but expressing his desire not to use it unless required. In any case, he was not lord—that was the prerogative of the Lord Jesus Christ alone. He would not "lord it over" others as if he were the Christ. His authority was derivative and a stewardship (cf. 13:10). It was conferred upon him, by Christ. It is, then, important to wend your way carefully between the mere exercise of authority and its necessary use.

CHAPTER 2

1   But I made up my mind not to pay you another painful visit;
2   if I cause you pain, who will be there to make me happy except the same ones that I caused pain?
3   So I wrote what I did for fear that when I came I might be caused pain by the very persons who ought to make me glad. I am confident about all of you that what makes me glad makes you glad too.
4   It was out of much affliction and anguish of heart, and through many tears that I wrote to you, not to cause you pain, but rather, to let you know the fullness of love that I have for you.

What does Paul mean by "sparing" the Corinthians (v. 23)? He explains in verses 1-4. The word translated "spare" has the idea of "turning back" from something or "refraining" from doing something. By a deliberate decision based on an intellectual judgment ("I thought it through and decided"—v. 1) he determined to bypass Corinth on his trips. This was because he did not want a repeat performance of what had happened in the past (2:1). It was not that he was afraid to be severe; when the occasion demanded it, he could be. But he wanted to give them time to work out their problems on their own (cf. 10:3-6). He had given them proper instruction; he wanted to see if they would follow it.

Paul certainly is not indulging the Corinthians; it is not a "spare the rod and spoil the child" situation. Even less is Paul backing out of a difficult situation for his own sake. As he maintains all along, it is the Corinthians' welfare that he has principally in view. A previous visit had been "painful" for both him and them (v. 1). Moreover, his letter had been pointed and sharp. It was not that Paul could not—or would not—face them; that he had done so previously makes that clear. He simply thought it best not to do so. They understood the apostolic word and how it applied to their problems. There was little he could tell them in addition. A visit would prove to be a time when he could do little more than scold them, and that was what he did not want to do.

"When you are pained," he says, "I am pained too" (v. 2). In such an encounter neither you nor I would benefit. And there would be no happiness in it. He wanted the next visit to be pleasant. And if, in time, they did make the necessary changes, when at length he did come, the visit would

5 But if somebody has caused pain, he hasn't caused pain to me, but to some extent—I don't want to put it too strongly—to all of you.

6   The punishment that the majority inflicted on this person is sufficient;

7   so, instead of going on with that, you should rather forgive and help him, so that he won't be overwhelmed by too much pain.

8   Therefore, I urge you to officially reaffirm you love to him.

9   This is why I wrote, to test you, to discover whether you would be obedient in everything.

10   Now, when you forgive somebody for something, I forgive him too; indeed, what I have forgiven (if I have forgiven anything), I have forgiven for your sakes in Christ's presence

11   so that Satan won't be able to gain an advantage over us; we aren't ignorant of his designs.

---

be a happy one (v. 3). So he wrote in great love, tears possibly staining the papyrus as he read it over when his amanuensis handed it to him for review.

In verses 5-11, Paul discusses the outcome of the case of discipline that was begun as the result of his first letter. In that place he severely criticized the church for allowing a case of unrepentant incest to continue right under their nose, undisciplined. He didn't ignore that problem, hoping it would work itself out. He was concerned that rather than "go away" it would leaven the entire church. He wrote them for the right reasons, in the right spirit—out of love (v. 4). But he had been severe; his words were sharp: he called the church "arrogant."

The pain that resulted from this confrontation was, says Paul, not principally mine, but yours (v. 5). Presumably his letter had its desired effect: they put the offender out of the church. And as a result he had repented. Now what should be done? To that question he addresses his present remarks. It will be instructive to learn what must be done when one put out of the church repents.

But first, look at some of the language involved. The "majority" is the first term. It is not, as some wrongly think, necessary to have a consensus in order to act. To wait for unanimity, in essence, is to submit to the rule of the minority who, if they want to, can forestall any and all action. No, Scripture is more sensible than that. The majority of whom? The elders, who represent the congregation in taking action and in ruling (cf. Ex. 19:7, 8 to see how the elders are equated with the people). In Matthew 18:19-20 it is two or three who gather together to put one out of the church. Note also the word "punishment." This is a peculiar word, meaning "disenfranchisement of a citizen." His rights of citizenship were removed from him. It was punishment of exactly that sort that was given in Corinth. The punishment, Paul says, is "enough" (*hikanos* = sufficient). Putting him out of the church brought about his repentance.

Now some wanted to continue to punish. Paul is more lenient: there has been "enough." Remember the elder brother in Luke 15; it seems there are always some like him. Now it was time to work toward restoration. There is forgiveness in Christ's church. Three important words are used to indicate how restoration is to take place: "forgive, comfort, reaffirm." The word for forgive is the one that indicates that a gracious, free offer of forgiveness must be extended to everyone who repents. The term "comfort" is (as in 1:3-7) the word that also means assist, in whatever ways necessary in each case. (Sometimes, since Satan can be rough, handing one over to Satan by putting him out of the church can have dire physical, economic and other consequences. The reclaimed brother or sister may need considerable "assistance" as a result.) "Reaffirm" is a word used only here in the New Testament. It means to ratify in an official way. It is an official pronouncement of one's reinstatement as a member of the church. The word was common in legal documents. It certainly calls for a formal, public announcement that the offender, upon repentance, has been readmitted to the full privileges of church membership. There was to be a formal declaration of the congregation's willingness to acknowledge the fellow-sonship of the repentant sinner and to extend to him fullness of brotherly love. It also implies formal records of such transactions.[1]

Counselors who faithfully exercise church discipline will find themselves devouring this passage. It is the locus classicus on the restoration of an offender who has been put out of the church. You should study it with great care to be sure that, in any church discipline of which you are a part, all the provisions for restoration are carried out and none is neglected.

In verses 9-11, Paul explains that he was testing their firmness in the faith by requiring them to exercise church discipline. He found that they were obedient in this matter—more obedient, indeed, than many churches today are. Forgiveness, he wants them (and, in particular, the forgiven offender) to know, is given all around—whoever they forgive, he forgives too. There are to be no loose ends; it is to be complete. Why should he forgive? Because the sin had caused him much pain. But if he (or they)

---

1. For more detail, see my *Handbook of Church Discipline*.

12 When I came to Troas to preach the good news about Christ, a door was opened for me by the Lord,

13 but my spirit has had no rest because I didn't find my brother Titus there. So I said good-bye to them and went ahead to Macedonia

---

went on nursing a grudge, it would be sin; Satan would gain a foothold. Unwillingness to forgive is something Satan loves to see. It creates division and continued hard feelings in a church. Forgiveness is, therefore, essential (cf. Lk. 17:3ff.).

What are Satan's designs with which it is important to familiarize one's self (v. 11)? Usually, as here, he attacks God's Word. That is what he did in the garden, creating doubt, leading to distortion and, ultimately, to denial. If some continued to hold off in forgiving, that would delight Satan. All the Corinthians, then, were to listen to these instructions (which were God's Word) so that in no spot in their church could Satan gain a piece of ground.

In counseling, from time to time it is important to properly (not in an exaggerated way) refer to the work of Satan because, in the refusal of counselees to do as God's requires, Satan's cause is advanced. Many counselees think that their failure to obey is only a personal matter. Not so. The entire church is affected. We are members of a body. When any part is adversely affected, the whole suffers. Satan gains a toehold in the congregation. That makes any individual's refusal to obey a church matter—not merely a personal one. The harm he does is not only to himself but also to the congregation of which he is a part. Never let counselees forget their corporate responsibilities. Part of your task is to restore them fully to their places in Christ's church.

Moving on to verses 12 and 13, Paul continues to speak of his concern for the Corinthian church. Even at Troas, where there were preaching opportunities galore, his mind was distracted: Titus hadn't yet come with word about Corinth, and he was concerned about the effect of his letter. A good counselor, though not allowing it to affect his work adversely, will carry his counselees' welfare on his heart. Paul did, though at the same time he entered the open door at Troas. You will always find that you must walk a narrow path between the two possibilities. You could become a white-coated professional with little concern at all (thus failing to "weep with those who weep") or you could undo your work out of overconcern. Be aware of what is happening to you. Once again, here is an area in which Satan's designs could trip *you up*.

14 But let me thank God, Who by Christ always leads us in His triumphal procession, and through us diffuses the scent of His knowledge everywhere.

15 To God we are the fragrance of Christ among those who are being saved and among those who are perishing.

16 To the one we are the deadly scent of death; to the other we are the life-giving scent of life. But who is sufficient for these things?

17 We aren't like so many who are peddlers of God's Word; but we speak like sincere persons do, like persons who in Christ have come from God and are in His presence.

So Paul went on to Macedonia. But not triumphantly—rather, as a defeated prisoner led along in God's triumph (vv. 14-16). As he thinks of his work as an apostle, he likens it to the spreading of the aroma by prisoners who, led in a great general's triumphal entry into Rome, were forced to waft incense along the route. Carrying the censors of the gospel's aroma from land to land, as one whom God had defeated and brought into submission to His Son, he preached a message that is the scent of life to some (the victors) and the scent of death to others (the vanquished, who would be strangled on Capitoline hill). These two groups present at the triumph he likened to those who believe and those who do not.

But handling the message of eternal life and death is too much for any man: Paul sighs, "Who is sufficient (*hikanos*) for such things?" In and of himself, no man is sufficient. No one should take the ministry upon himself. He must be called and supplied by God, Who alone can make one a "sufficient" minister of the New Covenant (cf. 3:6). Many who do take the ministry into their own hands determine to propagate the faith like a business (v. 17); they become "peddlers" of God's Word. They are not sincere; otherwise, they would not pursue the ministry for mercenary ends. Rather, like Paul and his retinue, they would appear as men whom God has sent. That is the way he wants the Corinthians to view him. And indeed, they should. How do your counselees view you? Is there room for suspicion?

CHAPTER 3

1 Are we beginning to commend ourselves again? Or, like some others, do we need letters of recommendation from you or to you?
2 You yourselves are our letter, written on our hearts, known and read by everyone.
3 And it is clear that you are Christ's letter, delivered by us, written not with ink but by the Spirit of the living God, not on slabs of stone but on the slabs of human hearts.

The third chapter has only 18 verses, but every one is personal. Paul is talking about his ministry. For that reason, we shall concentrate on those facts that pertain to the counselor himself. The first three verses introduce the issue—Paul's apostleship had been challenged. He must defend himself, not for his own sake, but for the sake of the gospel of Christ. The best defense is a good offense. Paul is on the attack. "I am not going to commend myself to you all over again. Why should I? After all, if I want a letter of commendation all I have to do is to refer to you, yourselves. *You* are my letter of commendation. Everyone knows that you were converted under my ministry and that, as a result, I have you on my heart. Indeed, you are a letter from Christ Himself, since He is the One who saved you. Who else can boast of living letters of commendation?"

Can you say as much of some in your ministry? Are there people whose lives you have so influenced that they could be referred to as such? The counselor, of necessity, becomes personal, very personal. That fact, properly handled, should endear him to those to whom he ministers. It should make him, perhaps, one of the closest persons in their lives. If people do not want to see or talk to you after sessions are over, there is something wrong about the way in which the sessions progressed. Sheep love the shepherd all the more for having rescued or healed them! Good counseling endears the counselee to the counselor, presuming all the time that the counselor has them written on his heart.

Paul had said that the ministry was too much for human ability (2:16). Every true minister of Christ will agree. Therefore if he was to carry on a successful ministry for the Lord Jesus he must draw upon a superhuman Source. In verses 4-6 He tells us about that. God is the Source of any competence he may have. Obviously God wants His ministers to be competent. Paul was **confident** that his ministry was *hikanos*

125

4 Such is the confidence that we have through Christ toward God;
5 not because we are self-sufficient, thinking that we could accomplish anything by ourselves, but rather because our sufficiency is from God.
6 He has made us sufficient servants of a new covenant, not of the letter but of the Spirit. The letter kills, but the Spirit gives life.
7 Now if the service of death, written in letters on stone, came in glory, so that the sons of Israel weren't able to look for any length of time at Moses' face because of its glory, even though it faded away,

---

("competent"). To be effective, a counselor must approach his work in confidence. Otherwise he will be hesitant, uncertain and doubting. That is precisely what counselees do not need. They have enough doubts and questions themselves; they hardly need the counselor's added to theirs! If the ministry is humanly impossible, how can anyone be confident? Only if that confidence is centered in the God who dwells within him. This is the counselor's hope. Yet it is the ground for the utmost confidence. If God is at work in both the counselor and the counselee, there is reason for the utmost confidence. Indeed, the Christian counselor is the only one who has good reason to have confidence at all. Both Rogers and Skinner at the conclusion of their lives gave up hope in their systems; they had failed to achieve what they claimed they would. Others have reached the same conclusion. Paul, in contrast, "kept the faith" till the end!

Human counseling schemes do not change counselees at a level of depth; only the Word of God ministered in the power of the Spirit does that. And we must ever assert that it does do so. The counselee, like these Corinthians, needs to know where the counselor's sufficiency comes from so that he will trust in God, not in the counselor. Only a Christian depending on God's Word can turn to never-failing promises. What you have, Christian counselor, is so superior to anything else in the field that you ought to chuckle with joy every time you think of how God has so adequately supplied and fitted you. And it is God who supplies not only instruction and knowledge, but also wisdom and know-how. God is the one you should trust to make you sufficient (v. 5). When others question your sufficiency, you should respond by agreeing that you are not so in and of yourself. But you do not counsel in and of yourself! You have a whole body of divine revelation on which you base your confidence. You have the promise found in that very revelation that God, who made and, therefore, knows men more thoroughly than anyone else, will equip you for ministering to your fellow believers (II Timothy 3:16, 17), and that He has sent His Spirit into your heart to help you learn and administer His

8   won't the service of the Spirit be even more glorious?

9   If there was a glory to the ministry that resulted in condemnation, the ministry that results in righteousness is infinitely more glorious.

10   As a matter of fact, what once was glorious, in this case, hasn't any glory when compared with the glory that so far surpasses it.

11   If what faded away came with glory, how much greater in glory is that which remains.

12   Therefore, having such a hope we can be very bold,

13   like Moses, who covered his face with a veil so that the sons of Israel couldn't continue to look until the final fading of the glory.

14   But their minds were hardened; to this very day, when the old covenant is read, the same veil remains unlifted, because it is by Christ that it is taken away.

15   Indeed, until today, whenever Moses is being read a veil lies over their hearts.

16   But whenever someone turns to the Lord the veil is removed.

17   Now the Lord is the Spirit, and where the Spirit of the Lord is there is freedom.

Word properly. Then you should ask him to tell you what he, or others, have as the basis for their confidence. You will find that he can put up precious little against what you have just outlined.

Now Paul moves on. Under the old covenant, in which the law was written on tablets of stone, the letter brought death because no sinner could find life by attempting to live according to the ten commandments. Every sinner failed. Paul's was not a ministry of urging people to keep the law for salvation. His ministry of the Spirit, given to God's elect, is a glorious ministry of life. His is a ministry to those who have broken the law. It is a ministry with a message that says "God will forgive and save sinners through the death and resurrection of Jesus Christ." That ministry is so much more glorious that the ministry of Moses and the law pales into insignificance when compared to it (vv. 9ff.). Indeed, that the ministry of Moses was less glorious was indicated by the fading glory on Moses' face. He covered his face so that the Israelites could not see it fade.

They should be able to see the difference, but their minds are hardened (v. 14). And they, like Moses, are veiled, this time with a veil that covers their hearts so that they cannot understand the writings of Moses when he is read (v. 15). They do not see Christ as the One about whom Moses wrote (cf. Lk. 24). But as soon as any one of them turns to Christ, the veil is removed (v. 16). Christ alone can take away the veil (v. 14). From these words it is clear that Paul considered his ministry as a glorious

18 All of us, with unveiled faces, seeing the glory of the Lord as if it were reflected in a mirror, are being transformed into His likeness from glory to glory, as from the Lord the Spirit.

---

one, superior to any other—even superior to the ministry under the old covenant. Why then should Christian counselors think that what God has given them is inferior, not only to that given in other periods of revelation but even to pagan concepts? Surely they who think so take quite a different view of the ministry of the Word than Paul did! Don't be ashamed of what God has given you, counselor. You are well-supplied.

Let me concentrate on verse 12 for a moment. Christian ministry of the Word should be not only confident but **bold**. The hope God has given for success is so great, it should inspire boldness in you. Look at the Book of Acts; throughout, the dominant note is boldness. *Parresia*, the freedom to speak without fear of consequences, here translated "boldness," is an outspoken, frank courageous utterance of truth. There is an unreservedness about it. Unlike Moses, who covered the glory, the veil is removed from the Christian counselor's mouth. How dare he cover the truth of God? It is absolutely essential for the counselor to tell it like it is. Much counseling, pastoral work and preaching fails right here. There is every hope of solving problems with a ministry so superior to all others. If God promises to make you *hikanos*, why shouldn't you boldly minister His Word?

Who is this Spirit who works with you in counseling? According to verse 17, it is the Lord Himself. And where He is, there is "freedom" to speak. No one need fear. So, with a ministry of unveiled face, you should not only radiate the glory of the Lord who dwells within, but become more like him in your ministry, as you are transformed into His likeness. Being involved in such a ministry should ever increase its glory as the Lord, the Spirit, makes you more and more competent (v. 18).

Thank God that as a Christian you are able to spend your time in prayer and the study of the Word. You do not have to ponder over the latest follies, fallacies and failures of the psychotherapists. People tend to grow into what they spend time thinking about. You may engage yourself in the study of that which not only makes you a more effective counselor, but also makes you a more holy person. What a privilege you have! Truly the ministry of the Word which saves and sanctifies is glorious! Never exchange it or dilute it for the sake of some other. What Paul is saying is that there isn't anything that even begins to compare with it.

CHAPTER 4

1 Therefore, since we have this service to perform as the result of mercy, we don't give up.

2   Instead, we have renounced shameful, hidden activities, refusing to walk in craftiness or to adulterate God's Word. But by making the truth apparent we commend ourselves to every person's conscience in God's sight.

The eighteen verses of this chapter capture Paul as he continues to describe and defend his ministry. Our concern in studying them for their counseling insights will focus upon the remarkably instructive explanation of how it was Paul could endure the afflictions to which he was subjected without despair or depression. From an understanding of this, you will be able to help many persons who have fallen into difficult times but have no idea of how to avoid depression. This is a counselor's chapter, *par excellence!*

What is it that impelled Paul to carry on? A quick review of the afflictions listed in chapters 6 and 11 once more points up the fact that he continued his work despite the most adverse circumstances. And that is precisely how he opens the discussion in the fourth chapter. He says **we don't give up.** The King James version reads "we don't faint." But the modern English rendering is true to the meaning of the Greek verb and more clearly conveys Paul's meaning today. It means "to despond through fear." There is always something of a note of cowardliness in depression. One is afraid to face the future, has given up the battle, surrenders to the enemy. A depressed person is saying, "I can't go on, I can't stand any more, people would be better off without me." There rings in it a clear note of surrender. All of that is present in the Greek verb used here (and in v. 16) by the apostle. Suicide, often connected with depression, is also the coward's way out. Thinking only of one's self—not caring for the consequences in the lives of others who remain—the suicide (failing to reckon that this life is not all) determines to step off the globe because he "can't take it any more." If the world is not turning out to be his oyster, well....

Simplistic schemes of analyzing and handling depression rightly note that difficult times and incidents or periods (what I shall call "pressures") usually precede depression, but then, in a *post hoc propter hoc* manner, conclude that these are the **cause** of it. But Paul continually faced

3   So if our good news is indeed veiled, it is veiled to those who are perishing,
4   to unbelievers, whose minds the god of this age has blinded to keep the
illumination of the good news about the glory of Christ (Who is God's
Image) from shining upon them.
5   We don't preach ourselves, but Christ Jesus as Lord and ourselves
your slaves for Jesus' sake.

---

hard times (remember chapters 6 and 11), yet here, he affirms that he did
not "give up." How was it that the apostle was able to face every kind of
affliction yet not become depressed? Obviously simplistic views are
wrong because they posit only two factors: *stress*, leading to *depression*.
But there is a third, and that is the secret to avoiding depression and to
getting out of it should one become depressed. That third factor, standing
between the other two, is *how one handles pressure*. The great variable is
how one responds to pressure. Paul did not become depressed because he
had learned to handle affliction and trouble God's way. Those who do, do
not need to become depressed. He could write, "We are afflicted in all
sorts of ways, but not crushed; perplexed, but not given to despair" (v. 8).
Even the most extreme pressures did not lead to depression.

What was it that made the difference? The clue that leads to the
answer is found in the first part of the first verse: **Therefore, since we
have this service to perform as the result of mercy**, Paul says, "we
don't give up." His gratitude to God impelled him to continue in the service (ministry) to which He had called him, no matter what happened. He
knew that he deserved nothing from God but wrath. How grateful, therefore, he was for the mercy that had been shown him in pure grace, not
only saving, but also putting him into the service of Christ in such a prominent way. Because of that gratitude he would carry on his ministry to the
end. He would continue, though left in a pile of stones for dead at Lystra,
though shipwrecked, though lashed, though imprisoned... He would continue to preach the gospel world-round until his Lord said "enough." He
was wholly at the beck-and-call of the One who had called him in the first
place. Cowardice faded under the bright light of gratitude.

Now what are you to make of that in dealing with depressed persons?
Simply this: those who follow their God-given tasks (whatever they may
be: homemaker, teacher, preacher) rather than their feelings will not
become depressed. And those who have trouble doing so need once more
to remember the pit from which they were taken. They need a new dose of

6   Because the God Who said, "Light shall shine out of the darkness," is the One Who made it shine in our hearts to bring to light the understanding of God's glory in Christ's face.

7   But we have this treasure in clay pots so that the surpassing greatness of its power may be God's and not ours.

8   We are afflicted in all sorts of ways, but not crushed; perplexed, but not given to despair;

9   persecuted, but not deserted; struck down, but not destroyed;

---

gratitude not only for their salvation, but also for the task that He has called them to perform—however mundane, no matter how difficult the consequences. Those who have already become depressed, similarly, will pull out of their depression only when they stop following their feelings and thankfully take up their God-given responsibilities once again.

Then, too, there was no personally-caused stress that might tempt him to become depressed. In verse two, Paul describes the sort of ministry in which he engaged: it was a ministry of sincerity and truth. He did not become entangled in things that pricked his conscience: his conscience was clear before men and God. Unlike others, he avoided all craft, hidden and shameful activities, and refused to adulterate God's truth with eclectic views. In short, he was genuine. In Paul, what you see is what you get. He had no hidden agenda. He was straightforward, frank and honest. Such a life-style leads to strength and fortitude rather than cowardice. It steers one away from the temptation to give up. But of course, if one should succumb, it is always possible to get out of depression by repenting of the sin and following the task again, this time in sincerity and in truth.

So, Paul says, because I am up front about everything, if anyone has difficulty understanding, it is because *he* is wearing a veil, not because (in some fashion or other) the message is veiled. And of course that is precisely the problem in trying to counsel unbelievers: they can't "see" the truth because they wear a veil over the eyes of their hearts. It is useless to attempt to counsel the lost. Since those who are in the flesh "cannot please God" (Romans 8:8), even if you achieved change it would only amount to a new life-style that was equally displeasing to God—or more so. So remember, the only constructive thing to do for unbelievers is to do good to them and present the gospel to them. Never try to get *them* to do good—they can't. Verse 4, perhaps, says it most powerfully: Satan has **blinded** them **to keep the illumination of the good news about the glory of Christ from shining upon them.** Their thinking is all messed up (notice vv. 3:14 and 4:4 where the mind is said to be wrongly influenced

10   always carrying around the death of Jesus in our bodies so that the life of Jesus might appear in our bodies.

11   We who live are constantly being handed over to death for Jesus' sake, so that the life of Jesus might appear in our mortal flesh.

12   So then, death is at work in us, but life in you.

13   Since we have the same spirit of faith as the one who wrote, "**I believed; therefore I spoke,**" we too believe, and therefore we speak,

---

by the evil one). An unbeliever cannot think God thoughts after Him. (Cf. my discussion in I Corinthians 2.)

Ultimately there are only two messages: what man thinks and what God thinks. In verse 5, Paul says that He preaches only God's message. Of course, the problem today, as then, is that there are those who falsely make the same claim; while purporting to preach God's message, they go about with some other humanly-concocted scheme dreamed up on their own or borrowed from others. That is the plague of counseling in our time. People by the buckets claim to be doing *Christian* counseling when all the while they are spouting forth something else that, at best, is a mixture of truth and falsehood. The glory of the ministry of God's Word is to proclaim Christ, the One in whom alone truth shines forth. He, no one else, is "the Way, the Truth and the Life." How Christian counselors can turn to Freud, Ellis, Maslow, Rogers and Skinner, whose faces exude no glory from the glory of God shining in Christ's face (v. 6), is hard to understand. After all, it was not the glory of Freud, *et al.*, that shone in their hearts when they were converted! Light and understanding about life come from God—not from sinful men, no matter how ingenious their theories may seem.

And it is interesting to note Paul's attitude toward himself as he engaged in ministry: the treasure was everything; the vessel that contained it, nothing. That is the proper approach one must have to the work of Christ. It is easy for a counselor to become puffed up and proud. How important it is to see himself as Paul did—as nothing more than a container for God's truth. And notice, the container is a clay pot, not some valuable vessel of silver or gold. That means that when counseling, Paul saw to it that Christ, not he, received all the credit for anything good. He always made it clear that it was by the power of God, not his own cleverness, that good came about. That is not always true of counselors today. How about you?

14 knowing that He Who raised the Lord Jesus will raise us also with Jesus and will present us with you.

15 Now all of this is for your sake so that as grace spreads to more and more people, it may result in an overflowing of thanksgiving to God's glory.

16 As a result, we don't give up, even though our outer person is decaying, because our inner person is being renewed daily.

I have mentioned verse 8 earlier but it is, perhaps, important to say just a word more about this all-important verse. Paul was often "down," but not "out." He was, at times, weighed down with the load, but not **crushed.** At times **perplexed, but not given to despair.** There are times when, from sickness, problems or whatever, we get "down," but that is not depression. Depression is when you are "down and out." That is to say, when you give in to your feelings in a down period, then it is that you find yourselves sliding into despair (depression). Depression comes from handling a down period wrongly. If in a period of adverse feeling you give *in* to those feelings you will soon give *up* on your responsibilities. Whenever you are down, for whatever reason, watch out. That is the time to adhere to your responsibilities all the more closely. That is also the time to remind yourselves of the goodness and mercy of God. God will not abandon you (see v. 9).

These are the sorts of facts that need to be reiterated again and again in counseling. Depressed people must be encouraged to do what they physically can do (but do not feel like doing) *in spite of their feelings.* Often on a homework sheet I will write, "Do so-and-so [whatever it is they have neglected] NO MATTER HOW YOU FEEL." That is the key, so long as they do it out of gratitude to God.

Paul says his ministry exposed him to the same sort of sufferings that Jesus' did (v. 10). Persecution and death loomed before him at all times as if he carried them around with him. Well, you may not face persecution and death every day, as Paul did, but you will certainly face misunderstanding and ridicule. The way God snatched Paul from the jaws of death was almost like a resurrection to the new life of Jesus. That is why he could say that again and again he suffered not only persecution but deliverance (v. 11). But this very "death" in him was what brought life to them.

Troubles, the "death" of many persecutions, do not keep me from preaching the truth to you, Paul says. As the saints of old, Paul believed and **therefore** spoke. His ministry was predicated on the truth of what

17 This temporary light affliction is producing for us an eternal weight of glory that is beyond all comparison,
18 since we aren't looking for the things that are seen, but rather for the things that are unseen. The things that are seen are temporary, but the things that are unseen are eternal.

Christ had done. It was a ministry of conviction. He viewed it not as a job, but as a work of gratitude for the greatest thing that had ever happened to him. No one should carry on ministry from a lesser motive. And indeed, God responding by his many "resurrections" from near death encouraged him (v. 14).

Why didn't Paul "give up?" Verses 15 and 16 explain once again from a slightly different angle. He ministered because he wanted to thank God for all He has done. As men were converted and blessed, that redounded to God's glory and was a way in which thanks could be expressed. That is why he could continue on even though his body was deteriorating. Paul was literally coming apart at the seams. He went on, never giving up, because God gave him joy and hope internally every day through the blessings that accrued from his ministry to others. This renewed him and drove him on.

Paul was engrossed in the ministry of the present and gave himself unstintingly to it, but he also never took his eye off of eternity. That is why he could make the comparisons listed in verse 17 and say what he did in verse 18. Paul can call the afflictions he endures **temporary and light**. But only in comparison to the **eternal weight** of glory. By faith he saw not only the temporal and visible, but also the eternal and invisible. That, too, helped him go on. Counselors must help counselees focus on the eternal results of temporal activities. Only then will they gain the proper perspective on the present. If Paul could call his trials "light," so can your counselees!

This is a powerful chapter for counselors. It would be well for them to spend many hours gaining an understanding of all of the nuances of the chapter that it was not possible to include here. Turn to it often. Turn to it *every* time you discuss depression.

CHAPTER 5

1 Now we know that if the tent that is our earthly house is destroyed, we have a building from God, an eternal house in the heavens that hasn't been made by hands.

2   So indeed, we are groaning in this one, longing to put on our house from heaven,

3   so that by being clothed with it we won't be found naked.

4   Yes, we groan under the oppression of it while we are in the tent—not that we want to put it off, but rather that we may be clothed in such a way that what is mortal may be swallowed up by life.

Having mentioned the present sad condition of his body (4:16) and the eternal weight of glory that he was looking forward to, Paul thinks about the radical changes that will occur at death and the resurrection. The **tent** in which he now dwells is his body. He contemplates its eventual destruction. But in the resurrection he knows that he will receive a newly-fashioned body that God Himself will give him that will be eternal (v. 1). Counselees suffering from physical ailments, like Paul, should be comforted by thinking of the present body, together with all its ills, as temporary (it is like a tent). The eternal body that will be given after the present tent is folded up and discarded will have none of those imperfections.

But that day has not yet arrived (v. 2). We continue to groan from pain and other infirmities in the present body. Groaning is not wrong so long as it has the proper effect. Present suffering should lead the Christian to long for the new, heavenly body God has promised. After a period of disembodiment at death, when we are (to change the figure of speech) naked—having put off the body—the day of reclothing with the new body will occur (v. 3). Existence after death, when the spirit leaves the body (cf. James 2:26), is an unnatural state for man, who was intended to dwell in and function through a body; death, prior to the resurrection, is therefore looked on as if it were a state of nakedness. But the time of reclothing will come.

Mixing the metaphors of clothing and dwelling in a tent, Paul says that though groaning in the tent, we don't find it easy to put it off (i.e., die and enter a state of disembodiment). That is not the state we look forward to. Rather we anticipate the reclothing of our spirits with an immortal

5 For this event God, Who gave us the Spirit as a down payment, has prepared us.

6   So then we are always confident, knowing that while we are at home in the body, we are away from the Lord;

7   we walk by faith, not by sight.

8   We are confident, then, and would prefer to leave the body and go home to be with the Lord.

9   So then, whether at home or away from home, we make it our ambition to please Him.

(deathless) body (v. 4). That is the hope of the Christian—not death (things are not finalized then), but the resurrection when all things finally will be righted. By giving us the Holy Spirit, who is beginning to work in our lives to assure us and to remold us into the likeness of Christ, God is preparing us for that eternal existence. He is the downpayment on the heavenly state Christ purchased for us. We are confident about the future even though we are at home in our bodies and absent from the Lord (v. 6). So our present manner of life (**walk**) is by faith not by sight (v. 7). We do not yet see the Lord or experience the joys of resurrected living, but we look forward with certainty and joy by **faith**. Does your counselee have that true and ever-present expectation in trial? Do you need to remind him? Does he need hope rekindled? That is an important aspect of biblical counseling.

Even though temporarily we will be unclothed at death, when we think of Him we would prefer to leave the body behind and go to be *with the Lord*. Then we will be tenting in a foreign land no longer; we will be **at home.** But either way, serving Christ here or there, our ambition is to please Him (vv. 8, 9).

What a profoundly simple explanation of Paul's hope. This, as it should also do for your counselee, impelled Paul to continue his ministry despite the sorry condition of his battered and bruised body. Sooner or later, most of us groan with the weight of worn and poorly-functioning bodies that increasingly fail us. Few passages should bring as much hope to ailing counselees, who feel the weight of dragging about such bodies, as this one.

But, though subject to numerous ills, the body is important. We cannot blame our failures and sins on it because of its infirmities. We are to please Christ by *using these bodies* in His service. And the day is coming when God will judge the practices that your counselee engaged in **while he was in the body**. While there is conscious life, no matter how the body

10 All of us must appear before Christ's judgment seat, so that each may receive what is coming to him for the practices in which he was engaged while he was in the body, whether they were good or worthless.

11 Therefore, knowing about the fear of the Lord, we persuade people; and what we are is apparent to God, and I hope is apparent to your consciences also.

12 We aren't commending ourselves to you again, but are providing you an occasion to boast about us, so that you will have an answer for those who boast about the outward appearance and not about the heart.

---

is injured and worn, there are ways of using it that please Christ. Sometimes that will take creative thinking to determine how. But in all things this should be the "ambition" of every Christian. In all the work that a counselee does he is called to do it not for his own benefit or for the benefit of others principally, but *to please Christ*. That means that he can do many things that he doesn't want to do, doesn't feel like doing or fears doing—just to please Christ. Remind him of that when he claims he "can't." Though he may not wish to do a thing he should always wish to please Christ who, though He did not wish to go to the cross, did so *for him*. And on the day of judgment, Christ, seated on His throne, will hand out rewards and losses according to how he used the body (v. 10). Unbelievers also will be judged on the deeds done in the body but with reference to degrees of punishment rather than rewards.

The body is the instrument with which we may glorify God; and it is not to be deprecated, but utilized for the purpose for which it was given. Humbled though it may be by sin, wrongly habituated by the sinful nature with which we all are born, it is our duty so long as we live in this tent to bring it into the service of Christ. Those who are "ambitious to please Him" will make every effort to do so.

Knowing how fearful it is to fall into the hands of the living God apart from Jesus Christ (this point was raised by the thought of unbelievers receiving the sentence of eternal death at the judgment), Paul says he *persuades* people. That this is his concern and that he is genuine about it, he hopes is as apparent to others as it is to himself (v. 11). A large part of counseling, like witnessing, is persuading people. But it is not sophistic persuasion that Paul has in mind; it is persuasion from the Word of God.

Since he has been attacked, he must say more about his ministry. To do so is not to commend himself. Rather, he is concerned to give them facts about which they can "boast" to those who oppose. Then they will be able to confute those who are concerned only about outward appear-

13 If we have taken leave of our senses, it is for God; if we are in full possession of our senses, it is for you.

14 The love of Christ is our motivation, since we judge as follows: One died for all; therefore all have died.

15 He died for all so that those who live might live no longer for themselves, but rather for the One Who died and rose for them.

---

ances and not about inner realities (the heart v. 12). If this procedure seems madness to them, so be it; it is madness for God's sake. If it seems reasonable; all the better. There is reason enough for Paul and his team to defend themselves, not for their own sakes, but for the sake of the Corinthians (v. 13). Here is another place where motives could be easily misunderstood. Recognizing this and taking pains to explain them is crucial. Learn from Paul's *continued* concern about such matters.

If you want to talk about motivation, says Paul, remember this: it is the love of Christ that motivates us. That is both the love that Christ gave (Romans 5:5) and that which subsequently is focused on Him. The former engenders the latter. This is a powerful verse. Counselees, for all sorts of reasons, should be called to examine their motives (you can't do it for them). Any motive lesser than love for Christ is wrong. Other motives are not wrong, per se, but if they supersede love for Christ they thereby become wrong. Take a practical example. A mother says, "I'll do anything to get my runaway daughter to return." She seems highly motivated. But watch out! Ask her, "Anything?" "Yes," she replies, "anything." Then ask, "Would you lie, steal, murder?" She answers, "Well, you know what I mean." Your answer: "No, I don't. I don't know where you would draw the line. Would you, for example, do all the things that God requires *as a gimmick* simply to get her back?" In other words, the mother must be ready to make any changes in her life that God requires, **whether her child returns or not**. She must put love for Christ even above love for her daughter.

The word used for motivation comes from the idea of being squeezed or pressed on both sides. It can mean "being pressed, and so carried along, by a crowd, or confined, channeled in a direction, etc." The idea, at any rate, is that there is a powerful impetus to direct and focus one's actions. Love, the only motivation that is more powerful than anger or fear, is the one that must motivate the Christian. Nothing else will do.

That love for Christ stems, of course, from His prior love to us, exemplified in His love shown by dying on the cross for the sins of His

16 So then, from now on, we don't evaluate anybody according to the flesh; although we did evaluate Christ according to the flesh at one time. But now, we don't evaluate Him this way any longer.

17 Accordingly, if anybody is in Christ he is a new creation; everything old has passed away; see, new things have come into being.

18 All these things are from God, Who reconciled us to Himself by Christ and appointed us to a service of proclaiming reconciliation—

19 that God by Christ was reconciling the world to Himself, not counting people's trespasses against them, and committing to us the message of reconciliation.

20 So then, we are ambassadors for Christ. As though God Himself were appealing through us, we urge people for Christ's sake, "Be reconciled to God."

21 For our sake He made Him Who didn't know sin to be sin, so that we might become God's righteousness by Him.

---

people. And all those for whom He died are counted to have died with him (see Romans 6). That means that they, crucified with Christ, may live in newness of life by virtue of being raised with Him. And since they have died to themselves—i.e., to their old self-centered life-style—they may now live for Him. Verses 14 and 15 are very useful when dealing with selfishness and pride. Verse 15, in particular, drives the rapier cleanly through the self-esteem, self-love viewpoint. It puts Christ before self at all points.

Verses 16 and 17 have to do with proper and improper standards of evaluation. What Paul says has powerful impact on both counselor and counselee. Paul has changed the standard by which he evaluates people. Before, he evaluated people by outer factors: sense perception, worldly standards, etc. (according **to the flesh**); now it is inner factors that make the difference. At one time, Paul even evaluated Christ wrongly. But now he knows differently. So people who are in Christ are not the same people they once were; they are new creations. They are becoming like Christ Himself. While he cannot know individual hearts, he must evaluate and treat a Christian differently; if genuine, a Christian is not the same person he was before. In this, there are many implications. What are some you can think of? Hint: they all have to do with hope and responsibility.

All change for the better in a person's life is from God (v. 18). This change comes about when one is reconciled to Him through the work of Christ; that message is at the very core of Paul's proclamation. His is a ministry in which people may find reconciliation and the forgiveness of sins (v. 19). And indeed, in a word, that is our message: "be reconciled to God" (v. 20). God, in punishing Jesus, counted Him to be the sinners that we, who now are reconciled to God by His death, know we were (v. 21). So in the last four verses he explains again the purpose of his ministry and the message that he proclaimed.

Does it sound like Paul is repeating himself? Well, he is. Though using slightly different words and phrasing it differently, he continues to hammer home his thesis: we are genuine and are engaged in God's ministry. Why? People forget. Others misunderstand. Counselees, often in a confused, troubled state, need to hear things said over and over again from several angles. Others still don't obey. They must be reminded of their failure. For these reasons (and more), don't despise repetition; it is often necessary. Learn to use it wisely when counseling. People forget!

CHAPTER 6

1 We also urge you as God's co-workers not to receive God's grace in vain.

2 He says, "**I have heard you at an acceptable time, and in a day of salvation I helped you.**" Don't miss this—**it is an acceptable time right now**; or this—**it is a day of salvation** right now!

3 We don't put stumbling blocks in anybody's way so that we may keep our service from being criticized;

In chapter six Paul continues to defend his ministry. Including the faithful Corinthians as "co-workers" in that ministry with him (an interesting concept when applied to counselees), he urges them to be sure that none of them has listened to the message of grace in vain. *Now,* he says, is the acceptable time to come to salvation, if by any chance some of you have not (vv. 1, 2). This parenthetical word shows how Paul never took the salvation of those who had professed faith for granted. It is conceivable that some of them *had* received the grace of God in vain—i.e., may have made a false profession. While we do not challenge the genuineness of a counselee's Christianity because it is impossible to read his heart, if he refuses to obey biblical injunctions, after adequate instruction and help, it is never wrong to raise the question of salvation as one into which it may be profitable for him to look. That is what Paul was doing here. The attack on him had been severe enough to make him wonder about the faith of some.

Some, possibly, had developed doubts about the gospel that Paul preached after the attacks upon his person began. It is for that very reason that Paul is at present in the midst of an elaborate defense of his ministry. To many, the faith and those who proclaim it to them are too tightly bound together. For them, the two stand or fall together. That Paul understood this human tendency to entangle the two is clear. He says that because he understood this he was careful to do nothing that would become a stumbling block to others. He zealously guarded his conduct so that it could not get in the way of anyone's faith. He would do nothing that would cause the ministry to be criticized (v. 3).

This broad statement of policy, growing out of this specific problem, is one for every counselor to ponder. Is there anything that you do that reflects negatively on the message of Christ (and ultimately, therefore, on

4   but as God's servants, we commend ourselves in all sorts of ways—by enduring much, in suffering afflictions, through hardships, under various pressures,
5   by being lashed, by being locked up, by going through riots, by laborious efforts, by sleepless nights, by going without food,
6   by purity, by knowledge, by patience, by kindness, by a holy spirit, by genuine love,
7   by a true message and by God's power; with the weapons of righteousness in the right hand and in the left;
8   through glory and dishonor, through slander and commendation, as deceivers and truthful persons,
9   as unknown and well known, as dying and yet—here we are—still living, as punished but yet not killed,
10 as deeply pained but always rejoicing, as poor but making many rich, as having nothing but possessing everything.

Christ Himself)? If so, you should take care to eliminate the practice, even if it is not necessarily wrong in itself. A stumbling-block is an unnecessary, man-made occasion for others to stumble over (i.e., to sin).

Now comes the first of the two lists of hardships that Paul endured for the sake of the gospel (the other is found in 11:23-29). It is a remarkable list, clear in itself, and needing no elucidation (vv. 4-10). What is to be noted is that Paul endured these things *because* his ministry was genuine. The argument is that no one would endure such things if he had not been sent by God and if his motives were insincere (see vv. 6, 7 in particular).

What can you, as a counselor, make of such lists? Well, I have mentioned already how useful they can be in comparing what Paul suffered with trials your counselee may be undergoing. By contrast, Paul, who did not complain, who all the more gave thanks to God's because suffering brought them closer, who stayed his course in spite of it all never becoming depressed, becomes an example of what a whining, ungrateful, defeated counselee ought to be—and can become. The lists expose the excuses of others as just that—nothing more than excuses. They also hold out tremendous hope. The counselee should be helped to say, "If Paul could so endure by the grace of God and that grace is available to me, I too can endure my significantly less taxing affliction."

Paul appeals to them. "Look," he says, "I have been open and frank with you; I've bared my soul. It isn't anything in us that has created a fro-

11 We have spoken freely to you, Corinthians; we have had wide open hearts.

12 You aren't being restrained by us; you are being restrained by your own emotions.

13 In response (I am speaking to you like children), open wide your hearts too.

14 Don't become unequally yoked with unbelievers; what do righteousness and lawlessness share in common? Or what fellowship is there between light and darkness?

15 What agreement does Christ have with Belial? Or what place does a believer have together with an unbeliever?

---

zen, sterile relationship between us. We have poured out our hearts. If there is hesitancy, it is on your part; you are the ones who have stifled your emotions. You have held back—come on, like good children, open your hearts to us again!" (vv. 11-13). There is a time to appeal to the emotions. Not apart from facts, but in the midst of them. We are not all logic, nor are we all feelings. The proper mix of the two, reaching the whole person, is properly called for in counseling as in all ministry. There are times to plead as Paul did here. There are times to spill your gut as he is doing throughout this very personal letter. But you must be careful not to do so in wrong ways and at wrong times. Use wisdom and good judgment always. But as a part of a long argument in defense of his character and ministry it was inevitable that at various points the emotional element would predominate. Few counseling sessions of any length and consequence will be free of emotional moments. Nor should they be. Don't become a white-coated, unemotional automaton; in counseling bring all you are and feel into the sessions (always keeping your emotions under control).

In verses 14-18, Paul strongly appeals to the Corinthians to depart from those who are unsettling their faith. Perhaps it was their old comrades whom they had abandoned when they became Christians, perhaps it was unsaved persons in the Church; we don't really know. But it is clear that it was unbelievers who had challenged the legitimacy of Paul's ministry. It would seem, from the passage he quotes in calling for separation from them, that the former rather than the latter was true. Either way, Paul makes every effort to break up the associations that were causing unrest. He warns about the unequal yoke of believers with unbelievers. He compares and contrasts them as opposites (vv. 14-16). Then, in the words of

16 In what way can God's temple and idols reach common consent? Now we are the temple of the living God. As God said,

> **I shall dwell with them and walk among them,**
> **and I shall be their God**
> **and they shall be My people.**

17   **So then, come out from their midst and be separate,**
> **says the Lord,**
> **and don't touch unclean things.**

18   **Then I shall welcome you**
> **and I shall be a Father to you,**
> **and you will be My sons and daughters,**

says the Lord Almighty.

---

the Old Testament, he calls them to come out from among such persons and be separate. When they do, they are really leaving nothing behind; God Himself will welcome them (vv. 17, 18). What have you left when, by doing so, you enter into the family of the heavenly Father and become his child?

In the first letter, Paul warned that evil companions corrupt good habits (I Corinthians 15:33). Evidently that warning had not been heeded, at least by some. Here a more direct appeal is made in very strong terms. There are times when the influence of other persons, usually not believers, is so strong that the only way to begin to make headway with a counselee is to call on him to abandon those who are pulling him in the wrong direction. In data-gathering, therefore, it is important to check out who are the influential persons in the counselee's life and to discover what advice they are feeding him. Also a sketch of their life-styles, what the counselee does in conjunction with them, and an analysis of their opinion of Christ and Christian counseling might be informative. The counselor who is alert to such matters, always filling in the context of a counselee's life so as to understand the factors that impinge on his behavior, will seldom go wrong in making such an appeal.

CHAPTER 7

1   Since we have these promises, dear friends, we must cleanse ourselves from every pollution of flesh and spirit, completing our holiness out of fear for God.

The word translated "pollution" in verse 1 can mean "to smear over with filth." That is what God thinks of our sin. In a sense, all ministry is a process of cleaning up God's smeared children so as to make them more acceptable to Him. Counseling is one part of the ministry of cleansing. Here it is the individual Christian that Paul exhorts to **cleanse** himself. But, as every counselor knows, that is precisely the problem—when left to themselves, many Christians fail to do so. Usually their failure is the result of ignorance (they don't know how) and/or unwillingness. The biblical counselor wrestles with both.

God wants perfected Christians, those who are **completed** in holiness. Perfection in this life, in the sense of sinlessness, is impossible. However, perfection in the sense of completeness is attainable. By completeness is meant that *a Christian is working on every aspect of his life* to cleanse it from filth and to perfect holiness in it. He wants to "lack nothing," as James puts it. It is the task of the counselor to help him become a *teleios* or "complete person" (James 1:4). The corresponding Hebrew word, found in Job 1:1 for instance, is *tam*. Both the Hebrew and the Greek words indicate someone who "has it all together." He is not sinless in any area of his life, but he is working on *every* area in order to bring it more and more into conformity to the Word of God. He is growing *across the board*.

Because God wishes this, it is the counselor's task to deal with more than presentation problems initially introduced by the counselee. As he progresses, if he uncovers other problems, at the minimum, he is obligated to point these out as well. And while he may not find it necessary or possible to take on every problem uncovered in every counselee, he may wish to tackle others besides those presented. At the very least he should inform the counselee of other difficulties that need to be encountered by him. It may be that, once aware of these, they can be handled by the counselee himself without help from another brother. But that does not mean that counselors may avoid dealing with interdependent problems. Some presentation problems are only solvable as previous ones are first dealt with.

That there are two aspects to every difficulty is certainly pertinent. Neither side may be discarded in favor of the other. Paul speaks of being cleansed **from every pollution of flesh and spirit.** That statement indicates that sin has a double face. Sin has corrupted both body and spirit. Man is **totally** depraved. That means that he has been corrupted in his internal self (variously described as "heart, soul, mind," and here as "spirit"[1]) as well as in his body. The spirit (the nonmaterial part of man viewed as independent of the body) ought to be the leading or ruling aspect of man. However, since it is corrupted it leads astray, and allows the body to do what it should not. It needs to be purified so that the Christian thinks and reasons and wills according to the Scriptures. The body too often takes the lead. It too has problems. Not only is it affected by sin in terms of defects and infirmities but sin dwells in its members (cf. Romans 6, 7). By that Paul means the body has become habituated to sin. The sinful nature within, with which man was born, has programmed the body to act under certain circumstances automatically, smoothly, comfortably and unconsciously in sinful ways.

This twofold nature of every problem faced by the counselor requires a double counseling response. The counselor must not only elicit agreement to the biblical change contemplated and an inner determination to work on it, but he must spend time helping the counselee to put this new way of life into effect. As the counselee is becoming rehabituated in some aspect of holiness (a process that takes at least 6 weeks of disciplined effort), the counselor monitors and corrects and, in various other ways, helps this process along. So there is an intellectual as well as a practical side to the process of change[2]. In the latter, the theoretical determinations reached by the former are transformed into reality. Probably as many counseling failures may be traced to the lack of aggressively encountering counselee problems on a double front as for any other reason. Neither the cognitive side nor the sensory one can be neglected. They must be faced and handled in tandem. Those who emphasize heart change alone are as much at fault as those who emphasize behavior alone.

In verses 2-8 Paul calls on the Corinthians to recall his ministry among them as they experienced it. He wants them to make room for him

---

1. See my book *A Theology of Counseling* for a discussion of these terms.
2. On this, see my *How to Help People Change.*

2 Make room for us; we didn't wrong anybody, we didn't corrupt anybody, we didn't take advantage of anybody.

3   I don't say this to condemn you, since (as I told you before) you are in our hearts to die together and to live together.

4   I have a lot of confidence in you; I have a lot of pride in you. I am full of encouragement; in spite of all of our afflictions, I am thoroughly delighted.

5 When we came into Macedonia, our fleshly bodies had no rest, but we were afflicted in all sorts of ways: fightings without, fears within;

---

in their hearts. After all, he didn't wrong or corrupt or take advantage of anyone when he was dwelling with them. Think, he says. Remember. It is so easy to forget when someone comes along with a plausible, sensational story and to allow less sensational events to fade into oblivion. But there were solid times together: conversions, lives transformed, blessings of various kinds. Corinthians—remember these!

It isn't my purpose to condemn you, says Paul (ever cautious that his words might have been overly cutting). You know that you are in our hearts, and so long as I live, right up till the day I die, you will remain there (v. 3). Nothing can dislodge you—even these attacks that have hurt so much. No, I'm not now condemning you; I believe that God has done a real work among you. After all He told me that he had many people at Corinth. You are His. I am confident of that fact. More than that I am proud of your church, despite all the problems. I am encouraged especially by things that I have heard about the changes you made since my previous letter. So even in the midst of such afflictions as I have described, you are an encouragement and delight (v. 4).

Most good pastors have something like these mixed feelings about their congregations. They love and admire their flocks for all that God has done through them, yet they see so much that needs to change. And that can be frustrating. The true pastoral spirit emerges in these verses. And any counselor who, in a stiff and formal way, deals with people without having them on his heart, without experiencing hurt and joy over them, is deficient. Biblical counseling is *pastoral*—i.e., shepherdly (reread Ps. 23; John 10).

In Macedonia, Paul suffered great afflictions. My physical body, he says, was worn out. I experienced fears within. Struggles of every sort. But when Titus came with word that there had been changes in you and that, by God's grace, you were coming out on the right side of things, this

6   but God, Who encourages the discouraged, encouraged us by the coming of Titus.

7   And it wasn't only his coming that encouraged us, but also the encouragement that he had received over you, telling us about your deep concern, about your mourning and your zeal for me, so that I was all the more delighted.

8 Even if I caused you pain by my letter, I am not sorry for it (though indeed I was sorry). I see that you were caused pain by that letter for a short time,

9   but I am now delighted—not that you were pained, but that your pain led to repentance. You were caused pain by God that you might in no way suffer loss by us.

---

buoyed us up like nothing else could (vv. 5, 6). God used this occasion to bring great encouragement.

What I am saying is that it wasn't just seeing Titus again that encouraged us—though that certainly was a great thing—it was the news he brought about you. How you had great concern, had mourned over your sinful ways, were zealous for my well-being. What a relief! What joy!

Now, says Paul, let's talk about the letter that brought about such changes (vv. 8-12). I know that I caused you pain by that letter. But I do not regret sending it, nor the pain that it engendered. Why? Well, first of all, the pain was short-lived. When you straightened out the many things that you did, it evaporated.

Stop! Did you get that? Paul didn't mind causing short-term pain in order to bring about long-term good. Many counselors, fearing immediate consequences, shy away from any painful advice or encounters. They thereby do short-term good (perhaps), but (certainly) long-term harm. Like any good dentist or physician, counselors must at times inflict short-term pain. Sin is the cause of the pain; the counselor only lances the boil. Healing, health, well-being is the ultimate goal. There is nothing sadistic in this, only love.

In fact, to go on, Paul says he was delighted that they were pained—because it had such a wholesome effect. He rejoices as the surgeon does when he sees the healing that the knife brought about. Their pain led to repentance.

Stop! Once more, let me emphasize a point. There are those who think change from sinful ways can be brought about apart from repentance. Not so. And for those who think there is no reason for a Christian ever to repent of sin, let him read these verses again! Paul's theology

10 Pain that comes from God produces a repentance leading to salvation that no one needs to be sorry about. But pain that comes from the world produces death.

11 Now, just look at the earnestness that this pain from God has produced in you; what a desire to defend yourselves, what indignation, what fear, what longing, what enthusiasm, what concern for justice! In every way you have proved yourselves to be innocent in the issue.

---

required repentance of Christians who needed to get their thinking turned around so that their living might also be inverted (again, repentance is the cognitive side that must occur along with the behavioral). God Himself, through my letter, brought about this pain. Because Paul was writing Scripture, he could view the effect of his letter as the work of God. He took no personal credit for it.

Because this pain was from God (it always is when a counselee is pained by the truth of Scripture winged home to his heart by the Spirit) it produced a repentance that led to a deliverance from problems ("salvation" is used here as it is in Philippians 1:19) that no one needs to regret. But when the world produces pain it leads not to healing and deliverance, but to confusion, sickness and—ultimately—death (v. 10).

Verse 11 describes the salutary results of the pain. It led to every kind of legitimate response according to the issue and the facts involved in it. There was earnestness, a desire to defend when they were wrongly accused, indignation against sin that needed to be dislodged, fear of sinning further against God, longing to see Paul so as to work out any remaining problems together, enthusiasm for what is right and concern for justice! I tell you, that is precisely what good, biblical counseling always produces. Perhaps in one of these cases more of one or two of these effects may be present. But in some respects, at least, all of these effects are present whenever counseling is blessed by good results. Take time to ponder each.

Stop! Elimination of pain is not the basic goal! That is what, in brief, Paul has been saying. The goal is *a proper relationship to God*. If pain is the only route to that goal, as it was in this case, so be it. Remember this, counselor. Pain is unpleasant for everyone; but, since as in disciplining a child pain is often necessary to peace and tranquillity, then one must not shy away from it. In the long run, it is a choice between immediate pain, leading to long-run peace, or present peace, leading to long-range turmoil and pain. Those who do not see and practice this are not ready to counsel.

12 So, though I wrote you it wasn't because of the one who had done wrong, and it wasn't because of the one who had been wronged, but it was in order that your eagerness for us in God's sight might appear to you.

13 As a result, we have been encouraged. Added to our own encouragement, we were all the more delighted over the happiness of Titus, because you all set his mind at rest.

14 Since I have boasted about you to him a fair amount, I was happy not to be put to shame, but just as everything that we said to you was true, so too our boasting to Titus proved true.

15 His emotions become all the warmer when he recalls the obedience that you all showed as you received him with fear and trembling.

16 I am delighted that in every way I can put my confidence in you!

Much of what a counselor does—especially in the early sessions of counseling—brings pain.

In verse 12, Paul makes it clear that he had no personal enmity against the offender who needed to be disciplined (that can be seen from his gracious encouragement to restore him; cf. Ch. 2). Paul made the decision to put him out of the church strictly *on principle* (cf. Lev. 20:11). And he makes it clear it wasn't even because of the one who was wronged by him that he wrote so vigorously; he wanted to get the church to turn around. It needed to be oriented in proper ways pleasing to God. This is what he wanted to **appear** in their handling of the situation. When that is exactly what happened, both he and Titus (who must have approached the Corinthian church with some trepidation) were thrilled (vv. 12, 13). After all, writes Paul, I didn't want Titus to be disappointed when he arrived at Corinth since I had said so many good things to him about you. All of our claims **to** you have proven true, just as all our claims **about** you have. And Titus was warmly drawn to you when he saw how submissive to truth you had become. How wonderful that I can put my confidence in you!

Throughout this letter and especially in this chapter, you have noticed how fully Paul commends the Corinthians *whenever he has a legitimate reason to do so.* That is important in counseling. Counseling that is all gloom and doom is unbiblical. Any progress legitimately achieved by counselees is fair game for commendation. After all, since pain is usually concomitant with counseling, it is important to lighten and balance this with as many good words as you can legitimately give the counselee. Commendation encourages. Use it freely in counseling. And teach those in multiple counseling cases (e.g., a husband and wife) to encourage one another in good works through the proper use of commendation.

CHAPTER 8

1 We want you to know, brothers, about the help that God gave to the Macedonian churches;

2 how in much testing by affliction, their abundant joy and their abject poverty overflowed in a wealth of liberality on their part.

3 I testify that they gave voluntarily according to their means, and beyond their means,

4 earnestly begging us for the privilege of taking part in this service to the saints.

5 They did this, not simply as we had expected, but first gave themselves to the Lord and to us by God's will.

Chapter Eight is a lengthy one, yet we can cover it rather quickly. Paul was raising a fund to take to the poor churches in Jerusalem. Many Christians had been disowned for their faith and others boycotted. They were under extreme persecution. Paul cared about these many small congregations scattered around the city. So he collected a fund from among the gentile churches to take to them. This was a love-gift to meet their needs.

Now he is about to mention this collection as he readies the Corinthian church to do its part. He begins by telling what God did among the congregations in Macedonia (v. 1). God so helped them that, in spite of the heavy tests and affliction they were experiencing for their faith, out of both abundance and sheer poverty (as the case may be in each congregation), they gave liberally to the fund (v. 2). Without any compulsion they voluntarily gave not only up to their means, but *beyond*! Indeed, it was they who begged—in all sincerity—to be allowed to participate in making up this fund (vv. 3, 4). We expected them to give something but they gave beyond all expectations. Why they even dedicated **themselves** to the Lord, and then to us according to God's will. In other words, they first gave themselves to the service of God and us, then, as a part of this general dedication, dedicated their gifts as well (v. 5).

Paul holds up an example of the giving of a persecuted church to encourage and stimulate the giving of one that was not. While not encouraging a spirit of rivalry, he did use the good example of one church to spur on another. Individuals known to your counselee who do not mind you telling about their own progress in overcoming problems may often be

6 So we urged Titus to complete the collection of this charitable contribution among you, because he was the one who previously began it.

7 But, since you abound in everything, in faith and in speech and in knowledge and in complete eagerness and in your love for us, see to it that you abound in gracious giving as well.

8 I don't say this as a command, but I am testing the reality of your love by comparing it with the eagerness of others.

9 You know the grace of our Lord Jesus Christ, that though He was rich, yet for your sake He became poor, so that by His poverty you might become rich.

10 So I will give you my opinion about this matter; it is to your advantage because you were the first not only to do something but to want to do so a year ago.

---

held out as encouragement to a counselee. "If so-and-so could overcome this problem (and you know how difficult his situation was), then by the grace of God so can you!" But always check first to make sure that anyone whose life you hold up as an example is willing to have you do so. And be sure that his example—closely examined—will hold up. Some counselees, rather than gain a benefit, will be quick to point out failures.

In verse eight Paul wades in. Now, Corinthians, I want you to give. But I am not going to **command** you because I want your giving to be spontaneous and willing. Titus, who began to take the collection, will complete it among you (v. 6). And I would like to see you give abundantly as those in Achaia did. After all, since God has given you an abundance of everything (v. 7), it would be appropriate for you to give abundantly out of that abundance. But I won't command this. Actually, in this offering I am testing how genuine your love is by comparing your eagerness to give with that of others.

Now Paul may not have commanded, it is true, but he did put pretty heavy pressure on them in that last statement. And that was not the heaviest, most impelling reason for giving. Next he lays it on them: Christ became poor to make you rich. He laid aside heaven's riches to give you the greatest gift of all—eternal life (in all of its varied dimensions both here and hereafter).

People must be encouraged to do God's will freely, not simply out of obligation. But it is not wrong to point out reasons for giving, even when they may, at times, constitute rather heavy pressure. To exert pressure *that is based on truthful and honest reasons* is always legitimate. But it must not be linked with a command.

11 Now, then, also complete what you must do, so that the eagerness of your desire may be paralleled by the completion of the task out of what you have.

12 Now if the eagerness is already there, it is acceptable for one to give according to whatever he has, not according to what he doesn't have.

13 I don't want to relieve others by afflicting you; rather, it is equality that I seek.

14 Your present abundance must be used to help those who lack in order that their abundance may supply your future lack, so that there may be an equality in sharing.

15 As it is written: **He who gathered much did not have a surplus, and he who gathered little did not have a lack**.

16 But thanks be to God for putting the same earnest concern for you in Titus' heart,

17 because he welcomed our appeal and has such earnest concern for you that he is coming to you on his own accord.

Rather than command, Paul will express his *opinion* (v. 10). Since you were the first to give to this cause, it would be appropriate for you to continue to take the lead in it. As long as a year ago you wanted to do something. By completing what you proposed then you will match your actions to your expressed desire. When the eagerness to give to those in want is present, it is proper to give what you can; I'm surely not talking about giving what you don't have (vv. 11, 12)! The idea isn't to impoverish you in order to meet the needs of others (v. 13).

In those words, Paul presents a sane, sensible approach to giving, not the wild, foolish approach heard so often in some circles. Some beg so strongly they would squeeze the last cent out of a person's purse if they could. What he wants is to level things out a bit (v. 13). After all, those now suffering want someday may be the very ones to supply those who are now abundant. The day may come when the tables are turned (v. 14). Quoting the ideal from the Old Testament (v. 15), he gives biblical evidence for sharing by those who have more than enough with those who have less.

I am grateful that God gave Titus the same deep concern for you that I have. He will work well with you when he comes. And I want you to know I neither asked nor begged him to visit you; it is of his own accord that he is coming. He loves you and wants to see you and minister in your midst. Notice, Paul takes the time to explain such things. Can you reason why he would do so?

18 Together with him we are sending the brother who is well thought of throughout all the churches for his part in the furthering of the good news.
19 And not only that, but he also has been selected by the churches to accompany us in the gathering of this charitable collection in which we are serving as administrators for the Lord's own glory and to show our eagerness.
20 What we want to avoid is for anyone to be able to criticize the service that we are rendering in collecting this abundant gift,
21 so we plan ahead to do well not only in the Lord's sight, but also in the sight of people.
22 With them we are sending our brother whose earnest concern we have tested many times in many ways, and who now is all the more earnest because he has such great confidence in you.
23 As for Titus, he is my partner and co-worker in serving you; as for our brothers, they are delegates from the churches, appointed to see that Christ is glorified.
24 So then, demonstrate to the churches your love and the truth of our boasting about you to these men.

Others (at least one of whom you and everyone else know well) will accompany Titus (v. 18). And this brother, who is known everywhere, has been selected by the other churches to accompany the gift that we as administrators are collecting all over the Mediterranean world (v. 19). Now Paul was concerned about money. It is a point at which people are quick to criticize. And, he says, I am zealous to see that this collection is made and delivered in such a way that everyone knows that everything about it is completely aboveboard. Therefore, to keep down any possible criticism, we are making plans ahead of time to do good not only in the Lord's sight (He knows our hearts), but also in the sight of everyone else (v. 21). That is why we have chosen a well-known and often-tested brother to accompany the gift to make sure that it gets to the people for whom it was given. And in addition the delegates from the churches and Titus will be there to make sure that all is done according to Hoyle (vv. 22, 23). Then, when all is open and apparent, Christ will be glorified.

How important it is to remain absolutely untainted when it comes to money. It is easy for people to make false accusations when large sums of money are involved. Many have, of course, abused their trust. That makes it all the more important to plan carefully ahead to make sure that all funds are properly used and that there can be no questions legitimately raised. Since counselors sometimes have to do with transactions involving money, over which counselees have been or might be fighting, it is important for them to teach their counselees to take elaborate precautions that will eliminate any possibility of suspicion. And counselors themselves must stay squeaky-clean when it comes to the handling of funds. To do so means thoughtful pre-planning.

So, Paul concludes, demonstrate to other churches both how genuine your love for the poor brethren in Jerusalem is, and that when we have boasted to them about your eagerness to give expressed over a year ago, we are not boasting in vain. Don't embarrass us; come through with flying colors! He will continue this theme in chapter nine.

CHAPTER 9

1 It is really superfluous for me to write to you about the service of the saints

2 because I know your eagerness. And since I told the Macedonians about you, saying that Achaia has been ready since last year, your enthusiasm has stirred up most of them.

3 Yet I am sending the brothers so that our boasting about you in this matter won't be in vain, but you will be ready just as I said you were.

4 Otherwise, if some Macedonians come with me and find that you aren't ready, we (not to speak of you) would be humiliated by our confidence.

5 So I thought it was necessary to urge the brothers to visit you beforehand and arrange in advance the bountiful blessing that you have already promised, so that truly it will be prepared as a bountiful blessing and not as something exacted under pressure.

Paul is still expressing his concern for the Corinthians' response to the offering for the poor saints at Jerusalem as we enter the ninth chapter. Surely if all you have to do in raising money is to pray and leave it to the Lord to provide then Paul's concern, his earnest solicitation of funds, and the careful arrangements he made were wrong. We cannot go along, therefore, with the "super pious" who advocate such things. It is pious to spend time at such matters, not to neglect them. People are wrong when they try to be more pious than Paul.

Of course, such things can be overdone. But the note, again, to hear ringing out crystal clear—a note unheeded by some in our day—is the note of care lest the ministry of Christ be criticized.

Paul is confident that the Corinthians will give liberally (v. 1). Their **eagerness** is the basis for that confidence. It was so evident that when he went to Macedonia Paul told everyone there about the enthusiasm he had seen at Corinth. And that enthusiasm stirred up the Macedonians to give. Paul says, "It would be a shame if, after having used the example of the Corinthians to encourage others, they gave freely but you saints at Corinth didn't; and if some of the Macedonians who will accompany me were to discover that all this enthusiasm of which I spoke was empty, I (not to speak of you) would be humiliated. That's why I am sending the brothers ahead. They can arrange everything ahead of time so that no such fiasco

6 Now let me say this: "He who sows sparingly also will reap sparingly; he who sows bountifully also will reap bountifully."

7   Each one must do what he has intended in his heart, not grudgingly or under compulsion, since God loves a cheerful giver.

8   God is able to give you more than enough of every sort of gift that you may always have enough of everything to abound in every good deed.

---

will take place. I don't want to have to come and take the collection at that time, having to put some sort of last-minute pressure on you" (vv. 1-5).

Prearrangements, concern, encouragement, embarrassment, confidence, planning—all these elements stand out. If Paul was anything, it was not sloppy. When something was to be achieved, he would do it decently and in order. Paul abhorred haphazard arrangements. He wanted things to be done with care—planning, then taking the time to do them well, thus avoiding many of the possible pitfalls that he could foresee. There is much to be learned here not only about how funds are raised and used, but how meetings should be arranged, how one ought to prepare for counseling sessions, etc. Think long and hard about the many implications of the concerns expressed by the great apostle in these chapters.

Verses 6 and 7 present a powerful incentive to give to the Lord's work. Sow sparingly, reap sparingly; sow bountifully, reap bountifully, says Paul. That is an important principle to remember in giving. Some counselees are tight, stingy. In a dozen ways in their dealings with one another and with their churches this becomes apparent. One reason why they have so few resources (physically and spiritually) is because they have been so miserly in giving. It is not wrong for a counselor to challenge them about their giving. No one can outgive God. He can point out the biblical principle of reaping and sowing. But it is not up to the counselor to tell anyone *what* to give. He may suggest, but the intention of the giver's heart must be his own. That is because God wants no one giving grudgingly but, rather, freely, cheerfully (vv. 6, 7).

Indeed, in return God is able to give more than one needs (v. 8), not just of money but of every sort of gift. When God returns what one gives it is not always in hard cash. Indeed, he may sow monetary, but reap spiritual, good (v. 10). Whatever He supplies, however, is enough to provide everything necessary to abound in doing good (v. 8).

In listening to the protest of those who do not always have as much money as they wish, it may be important to show them how God has repaid their giving with spiritual blessings—for example, the harvest of

9   As it is written: **He scattered, he gave to the poor; his righteousness continues forever.**

10   The One Who provides seed for the sower and bread for food also will increase your seed and will enlarge the harvest of your righteousness.

11   You will be enriched in every way so that you can engage in all sorts of liberality that through us will result in thanksgiving to God.

12   The service that you perform by this religious function not only meets the needs of the saints, but it also results in many thanksgivings offered to God.

13   By passing the test that this service provides you, they will glorify God for your obedience to your confession of the good news about Christ, and for the liberality of what you have shared with them and with everyone.

14   And they will pray for you with warm affection because of the surpassing amount of grace that God has poured out on you.

15   Thank God for His inexpressible gift!

---

righteousness that He has made available for their taking, mentioned in verse 10. Those who give to the poor—rightly (v. 7)—reap such a harvest (v. 9). And indeed, in all sorts of ways, God enriches them (v. 12). As a result, not only should the one who receives these bounties from God rejoice, but those who minister His Word to them should also (v. 11). God should receive the thanks of His people. "Your giving will lead to a chorus of praise from saints everywhere (v. 12). I have told you that your giving is a passing of a test of your genuineness. And the praise and thanksgiving that will redound to the glory of God as the saints at Jerusalem rejoice will only be the beginning. Thanking God for you, they will remember also to pray for you and God's blessings on you as well (vv. 13, 14). To end this discussion, let us never forget how much God gave. He did not spare His only Son, but freely gave Him for us. Let us ever praise and thank Him for that; for there is a gift so surpassingly great that human language cannot describe it." Why then should I try?

CHAPTER 10

1 I Paul urge you by the meekness and gentleness of Christ, I who myself am "humble" when I must face you but "bold" when I am away from you;
2 I ask you not to make it necessary for me to be bold when I am with you, as I surely count on being daring toward some who think we are walking according to the flesh.

Paul now turns his attention to other matters. He is still chafing from the attack on his ministry. Quoting those who scorned him he says, I am asking all these things humbly and gently as Christ would. But don't get me wrong, those who charge that I am **humble** when in your presence but **bold** when I am away from you don't know what they are talking about. What I am trying to say throughout is that I hope you won't make it necessary for me to be bold when I come—then you will discover how bold I can be! Indeed, I do plan to be bold toward those who have made charges that we are insincere (vv. 1, 2).

Counselees, when they do not want to make the changes that are required of them, may turn on the counselor. They may slander and falsely accuse him. In such cases, the counselor cannot remain passive. While it is proper to plead and urge, if every good attempt to help fails, and ends only in an attack on the counselor, it is time for the counselor to take strong action in response. Paul, like John (cf. III John 10), was willing to deal with all such insubordination to the authority of Jesus Christ, invested in His church. He would confront them—"boldly!" They would discover that Paul was not, as they charged, a coward after all. Many responses of counselors today are weak, perhaps cowardly. They don't want to engage in battles. They don't want to face people about their sin—particularly when venom is leveled toward them. But if one loves Christ and his church (not to speak of the offender himself) he will not allow sinners to go on confusing God's people with their unfounded accusations. He will respond powerfully.

Recently a minister told me about an instance where charges were made against him that were totally unfounded. He was asking his elders to set up a commission to investigate him to clear his name. I suggested that this was totally wrong. I insisted that rather than put the emphasis on himself, his elders should stand with him and refuse even to hear these

3   Of course we do walk in the flesh, but we certainly don't fight according to the flesh.

4   The weapons that we use to fight aren't fleshly; rather, they are divinely powerful to tear down strongholds.

5   By them we tear down arguments and every high barrier that is raised against the knowledge of God, and take every thought captive and bring it into obedience to Christ,

---

charges unless the accuser could present witnesses or other evidence. After all, Paul insists on this very clearly in I Timothy 5:19. His weak response tended to give credence to the charges (even though they were totally unsubstantiated) and could only lead to confusion and suspicion on the part of the members of the congregation. Paul would have faced this accuser, charged him with slander and called on him to repent.

He explains his approach even more clearly in verses 3-6. The ministry is war. It is not some pleasant 9 to 5 job. It is fighting the battles of the Prince of Peace against His enemies. Of course, says Paul, we are physical beings with physical bodies, but we do not use physical means to fight the battles of the Lord (v. 3). We don't attempt to achieve our ends by worldly methods. As Jesus Himself said, "My kingdom is not of this world, else would my servants fight" (i.e., take up physical weapons to further His kingdom). He did not imply that there were no battles to fight; what He was saying is that they would not use material means to wage war.

Well then, how should God's people (and you, counselor) fight? Warfare requires weapons—Paul plainly explains in verses 4 and 5. There are weapons to use in this war but they are not physical. Nevertheless, they are powerful—more powerful than any material arms: they are *divinely* powerful. That is to say, they are designed and used by God in His providence as they are wielded by His servants. They will effectively tear down the strongholds of the enemy. What are these weapons?

They are words of truth and light that expose the errors of those who oppose. They are powerful to defeat arguments and other barriers (emotional or otherwise) that enemies—or counselees—rear up against a knowledge of God. That is the sort of battle God's church wages. You have the most powerful weapons in the world to use against the enemies that have influenced your counselee. Don't ever lose sight of this fact or trade God's weapons for those of the world. Our weapons are powerful enough to take men's thoughts captive for Christ. That is one goal of the

6   being prepared also to deal justly with every act of disobedience, after your obedience is complete.

---

counselor: to rid minds of error and to bring the thinking of counselees into conformity to Christ's truth. But the cognitive side, once again, is insufficient. When one's mental obedience is complete (v. 6) that does not mean that he will automatically live and act as he should. That is why training in righteousness and church discipline also are needed. Unrepented acts of disobedience must be dealt with (v. 6). God, through Paul, is telling us that He wants an obedient people, as anxious and ready to live according to the truth as they are to learn it.

Counselor, ministry is war. You are a soldier fighting for the souls of men and women. You must view each counseling session as another battle with the enemy of men's souls. You are to win these battles by the use of the proper weapons, the weapons of truth found in the Scriptures alone. Like any good soldier, you must know your weapons. You must spend your time keeping your weapons in proper shape and you must learn how to use them effectively. The sword of the Spirit is the mightiest weapon ever devised; you must learn to use it well. Actually, it is the only weapon that God gave you.

In verse 6 Paul speaks of the importance of church discipline. Those who are taken captive for Christ must be disciplined into the new ways of His kingdom. Disciplined training must come first. But when it fails—because the counselee refuses to obey—the church must be ready to **deal justly with every act.** Discipline can be wielded unjustly against a counselee. He can be declared intransigent when the real problem is something else (e.g., discouragement, fear, misunderstanding, etc.). Punishment in such cases is *un*just. When one has submitted to Christ, by laying down his arms and coming to Him in faith, it is important to follow his life very closely. He has many changes to make—across the board. In every area, he must begin to think and handle matters differently. Otherwise the old ways from the past will harden in the new life. When he is newly converted, is experiencing that "first love" of which Jesus speaks in Revelation 2:4, he is malleable enough to make large changes quickly. And he is willing. If, on the other hand, he is allowed to become comfortable with the old ways of thinking and living after coming to Christ, later he will be much harder to move. Indeed, he may become comfortable enough that he does not want to change and may willfully disregard and disobey God's Word. That is when corrective discipline comes into play. I cannot delve

7   You are looking at the outward appearance of things. If someone is confident that he is Christ's let him think again about himself, that just as he is Christ's so also are we.

8   Even if I should boast too much about the authority that the Lord gave us for building you up and not for tearing you down, I am not going to be ashamed of it.

---

deeply into church discipline here, but I have dealt with the subject in detail in my *Handbook of Church Discipline*. The goal: every thought and action in submission to Jesus Christ.

Those who are disobedient and do not respond to church discipline positively must consider again whether their profession of faith is genuine (v. 7). The outward appearance can be misleading. If one is in Christ, then he will be like us, says Paul. If, however, he doesn't receive our message and recognize our authority, then his profession is doubtful. I do have authority from Christ. And I am not ashamed to mention it, says Paul. Why should he? It was given for but one purpose—to edify (build up the members of the church) and not to tear them down (v. 8).

Even church discipline carried to its limits (when justly administered) builds up. It always has as its ultimate purpose the restoration of the offender. That is why one must be "prepared" to use it. How important it is to know that the work of God's minister is to build up His people and that He has given him authority for this purpose. The ordained minister of the church of Jesus Christ has all the authority of Paul; indeed, as Paul did, he has all the authority of Christ! That is because his authority does not come from within; it is a conferred authority, given from above (*exousia*).

Other counselors who have never officially been called to the work of the ministry lack that authority. They may counsel informally, as every Christian is bidden to do, but they lack the authority to tell others to "obey." Christ's elders have the authority to do so (cf. Hebrews 13:17). That is why counseling as a life calling is the work not of some self-appointed person with psychological training and a smattering of theology, but the work of fully-qualified ministers of the Word. And all authoritative counseling must be done under the aegis of the church. It is wrong to go out and hang out a shingle somewhere, calling yourself a Christian counselor when what you do is not subject to Christ's church.

Paul has spoken about dealing with every act of disobedience and has called on those who are rebellious to take a second look at their profession

9 I don't want to seem to be frightening you with letters.

10 "His letters," somebody says, "are weighty and strong, but his bodily presence is weak and his speech is contemptible."

11 Let such a person consider that whatever we say when absent, we shall in fact do when present.

12 Of course we wouldn't dare to class or compare ourselves with some of those who commend themselves. But they aren't wise to measure themselves by each other and compare themselves with each other.

13 We won't boast beyond measure, but according to the measure that is determined by the sphere of activity that God has assigned to us, a measure that reaches far enough to include you.

14 We aren't overextending ourselves, as would be the case if we hadn't reached you; indeed, we were the first to reach you with the good news about Christ.

---

of faith. He will take action only after the efforts of the church and individuals in it are "complete." He realizes that this is hard talk, so he softens what he has to say—for the benefit of those who do not fall into such categories—by his words in verse 9. The purpose of my letters is not to frighten you, he assures them. After all, those who have been criticizing him have already made mention of his letters: they say, "his letters are weighty and strong, but when he appears in person, he is weak and his speech is contemptible" (v. 10). Well, will Paul let that kind of challenge to his God-given ministry go? You can be certain he won't! He has a word for his attackers: whatever I say in letters you can count on me to do when I arrive (v. 11). I don't want to compare myself with such persons; I have never commended myself the way they commend themselves. They can only do this because they measure themselves by the yardstick of others just like them (v. 12). If we want to measure ourselves let's use a more exacting rule: the measure of the kind of ministry that God has given us. And that measure reaches as far as you—you know what kind of ministry it has been (v. 13). If we were talking this way when we hadn't gone as far as Corinth, it would be a different matter. But we brought the gospel to you and you are well aware of the sort of ministry we exercised among you then, and have ever since. These people boast about what they can do for you, denigrating us, but unlike them we don't go around boasting about what we can do for a church that is the result of someone else's labors (v. 15). We worked among you and intend to continue to do so until our ministry to you has been greatly enlarged.

15 We don't boast beyond measure, about what is really the labors of others, but hope that, as your faith grows, our sphere of activity among you will be greatly enlarged
16 so that we may announce the good news in the regions beyond you rather than boast about what has already been achieved in another's sphere of activity
17 **Let him who boasts, boast in the Lord.**
18 It isn't the one who commends himself who is approved, but the one whom the Lord commends.

Don't try to counsel someone who is already being counseled by another. If the counseling that he is receiving is unbiblical, you should try to get him to leave it so that he may receive good counsel. But if what he is receiving is adequate, stay out of it. You have enough to do elsewhere. Listen to the principle embedded in verses 15 and 16 as it pertains to various aspects of counseling etiquette. Many people trying to counsel the same person separately causes nothing less than unnecessary confusion. And it may lead to rivalry.

These troublemakers at Corinth boast of what they will do for you. Don't listen to such drivel. If anyone wants to boast, let him boast about what God is doing. Whenever a counselor starts talking about *his* achievements, *his* effectiveness, etc., there is something regrettably wrong with him. Watch out. Any counselor who is worth his biblical salt knows that he is but an instrument in the hands of the Holy Spirit and that all glory for any good results belongs to Him alone. Moreover, if there is to be any commendation, even for being a faithful instrument, let it be the Lord Who gives it.

CHAPTER 11

1 I want you to put up with me while I indulge in a bit of foolishness; but, of course, you are putting up with me.

2   I am jealous over you with a jealousy that comes from God, since I was the one who brought about your engagement to one man, that I might present you to Christ as a pure virgin.

Paul is truly concerned about this attack on his ministry. He has already spent most of the letter dealing with the problem, but he is not finished yet. Here he tackles it once again, this time from a different angle. He asks the Corinthians to **put up** with him while he engages in some foolishness, saying, somewhat humorously, "but, of course, you are putting up with me." Clearly Paul is going to do something that he regrets having to do but can think of no other way of making his point. It becomes all the more vivid in the mind of the reader since Paul makes *such* a point of it. What he is about to do is to spill his gut to them and to recount all that happened in bringing the gospel to them. He is going to compare his efforts with those who have challenged his authority and shame them into silence. He doesn't want to do any of these things, but thinks it necessary.

There are times!

He begins by revealing all that he feels for the Corinthians. He is jealous over them with a godly jealousy—that is, a jealousy that is born out of the right motives and fits in with biblical concerns. I was the one who led you to Jesus Christ, he recalls, the One to whom I hope to present you as a chaste virgin (v. 2). But I am afraid for you. I don't want you to be deceived by these people who are upsetting your faith. I don't want you to be deceived as Eve was by the serpent. There is a cleverness that the enemy has about him.

Counselor, you too are fighting a shrewd enemy. You must not only become aware of his wiles, you must also know how to expose them to defeat him. That will happen only when you are fully prepared to reveal his ways to your counselee. The seductive nature of all sin is well-known to experienced counselors who, again and again, encounter Christians (who ought to know better) caught in the evil one's web. And when you try to extricate them they only become more and more entangled as they

3   But I am afraid that as the snake deceived Eve by his cleverness, your thoughts might be seduced away from simple and pure devotion to Christ.

4   If somebody comes and preaches another Jesus whom we didn't preach, or if you receive a spirit who is different from the One Whom you received, or a good news that is different from the one that you accepted, you put up with it well enough.

5   Indeed, I don't think that I am in any way inferior to these eminent apostles!

6   But even if I am unskilled in speech, yet I am not in knowledge; but we have made this clear to you in every way.

---

attempt to justify their sin. They have been deceived and go on deceiving themselves. You must learn to uncover that deceit so skillfully that there is no other conclusion to which the counselee can come but that he surely has been deceived.

Many of the deceitful ways of entrapping counselees come from the counsel of other Christians who themselves have been deceived into buying the views of pagan psychotherapists. Even after having left them, because they received little or no help, counselees may retain a residue of error to which they cling. It is often necessary to refute this error (what Psalm 1 calls "the counsel of the ungodly") before you can move ahead.

The simple and pure devotion to Christ of which Paul speaks in verse 3 stands starkly opposed to the clever views of men. Don't let your counselees be misled by those who claim biblical counseling is "simplistic." Simple, yes; simplistic, no. Truth is simple, because it is single. Error is complex, because it is multifaceted. There is only one way to be right according to the truth; there are many ways to be wrong. Moreover, truth simplifies; error complicates. If Nixon had told the truth about Watergate, he probably would have been able to retain his job. But lie plastered over lie led to such a complicated, tangled mess that the weight of its very complexity was what brought him down.

Paul is concerned because they are gullible. It seems that they will listen to anything or anyone. They had not learned the fact that truth is single. You can't hold to two or three contradictory "gospels." There can be only one true gospel. Yet they had been willing to hear views that contradicted the gospel that saved them (v. 4). Now, says Paul, these men claim to be **eminent apostles.** They claim superiority over us. They are super-apostles! Oh? Are they, now? How is it that I am inferior to them (v. 5)? Suppose they are smooth talkers—more skillful in presenting their error than I am in presenting the truth. That doesn't make them right.

166

7 Now, did I commit a sin by humbling myself in order to exalt you when I announced the good news to you without charge?

8 I robbed other churches by receiving a salary from them so that I could serve you.

9 When I was present with you and had needs, I didn't burden anyone; my needs were met by the brothers who came from Macedonia. So in every way I kept myself from becoming a burden to you, and I shall continue to do so.

10 As Christ's truth is in me, this boasting of mine shall not be stopped in the regions of Achaia.

11 Why? Because I don't love you? God knows that I do!

12 But what I do, I shall continue to do, so that I may take away any pretext for their boasting that they are doing what we are.

Consider *what* they teach. Is it superior to the **knowledge** that I have imparted? Surely not. But in all sorts of ways I have already explained this to you (v. 6). What is the problem then? Let's see; perhaps I committed a sin by humbling myself in order to exalt you, by preaching freely without charging you for it.

Pure sarcasm. Biting sarcasm—designed not to hurt, but to slice through the fog of confusion. If Paul, like these super-apostles, had tried to bleed them dry of their money, they could have reason to suspect his motives. But as it is he took a salary from other churches just so he wouldn't have to live off of the Corinthians (vv. 7, 8). That kind of contrast must have hit hard.

But he isn't finished. Even when he had needs (we don't know what they all were), he didn't burden them with them but received help from brothers from Macedonia. All this not to burden the Corinthians. And he plans still not to burden them with support for himself. As he believed the truth of Christ, so he believed he could continue this way so that the boast that he took nothing from those to whom he preached the gospel in Achaia could continue untarnished (v. 10). Why did I not take anything from you—because I don't love you? That's absurd; obviously I did this just because I do (v. 11).

I shall continue to take away the boast of these men that they too are apostles, carrying the same message in the same way that we are (v. 12). Now comes Paul's strongest indictment: These men are **false apostles** and **deceitful workers** .

13 Such men are false apostles, deceitful workers who transform themselves to look like apostles of Christ.

14 And no wonder, since Satan himself transforms himself to look like an angel of light.

15 So it isn't all that strange, then, if his servants transform themselves to look like ministers of righteousness. Their end will be in keeping with their deeds.

Look at each of these designations. False apostles. Apostles were "sent off ones." Christ had chosen and sent them as His ambassadors into all the world to preach the gospel and form churches of baptized converts. A false apostle is one who claims to be what he isn't. It is serious business to claim to be sent by Christ when one hasn't been. It is serious business to claim that one is doing "Christian counseling" when what he is doing is palming off the world's goods for Christian counsel. All he is is paint and smoke.

Such activities are deceitful. The deceit may not always be willful; one may truly believe a lie, but that doesn't make it any the less a lie. And if it is a lie, then it will deceive those who believe it. There is something, however, about the way in which much so-called "Christian counseling" is carried on. There are those who are openly eclectic. But then, there are those who carefully cover their wares so that you think that what you are getting is pure biblical truth when it is not. They represent themselves as engaging in "Christian" counseling when it is as plain as can be to one with discernment that what they are doing is using the views, theories and systems of unbelievers, then spray painting them with Bible verses. One man, for instance, presents the system of an unbelieving psychologist (who later committed suicide) and adds, at the end, a page of Bible verses! Others are more deceptive, calling what they do biblical when they themselves know that their systems are simply eclectic patchworks of unbelieving men painted up to look Christian. Though we certainly differ from them, we must respect more highly those who unashamedly admit that they are avowedly eclectic. The danger comes from deceiving people into thinking that they got their teachings from the Scriptures when they did nothing of the sort. The Scriptures were used as a thin coating to cover the basically non-Christian views beneath.

There is something Satanic about deceit, says Paul. After all, he began harassing the human race by *deceiving* Eve. Like Satan, these men in Corinth were disguising themselves as apostles of Jesus Christ. Satan is

16 I'll say it again: don't any of you think I am foolish; but even if you do, then receive me even as you would a foolish person, so that I too may do a bit of boasting.

17 What I say, I will not say the way the Lord would, but in a foolish way, in confident boasting.

18 Since many boast according to the flesh, I too shall boast.

19 Since you are wise, gladly put up with fools!

20 You put up with it if somebody enslaves you, or devours you or takes advantage of you, or snubs you or slaps you in the face!

21 To my shame I admit that we were too weak to do that!

But whatever anybody else dares to boast about—I am speaking in a foolish way, remember—I also dare to boast about.

22 Are they Hebrews? So am I. Are they Israelites? So am I. Are they descendants of Abraham? So am I.

---

smart enough to dress himself in Christian garb. He appears as an angel of light rather than as the prince of darkness. That's how one deceives another—not by revealing his true nature or what he is up to, but by making you think something else. These men Paul calls servants of Satan. While I would not go so far as to say that is true of all who misrepresent non-Christian error as Christian truth, one must conclude that their efforts have done much to ruin the lives of many people and confuse the church. In this way, unwittingly, they have played into the hands of Satan. For those who were preaching another gospel at Corinth, Paul predicts they will be paid liberally with that which they deserve for their evil deeds (v. 15).

Doubtless there were those at Corinth who did not like to hear such black-and-white things said. After all, wasn't there something good that can be said for these men? There always are those who will think and talk that way. But it is not a matter of sparing men, it is a matter of the truth and honor of God and the welfare of His church. Those were the impelling forces behind Paul's admittedly severe judgment on these men.

I hate to do it, I feel foolish to do so, but take me as you will—I too will engage in a little boasting (v. 16). That is how Paul introduces the next section. Everyone else is doing so; so here goes! And in your great wisdom (how that 19th verse drips with sarcasm!) you enjoy those who boast. So I'll do some boasting too. After all, you like others to enslave you, take advantage of you, snub you, slap you in the face. The trouble is, as they say, I'm too "weak" to do those things. (Oooo! Such juicy sarcasm.) I am ashamed to admit it. But, I'll boast the way they do (remem-

23   Are they Christ's servants? (I am speaking as if I were out of my mind) I am a better one. I have labored harder, been in prisons more often, suffered innumerable lashings, and have been in the jaws of death frequently.

24   Five times I receives 30 stripes from the Jews,

25   three times I was beaten with rods, once I was stoned; three times I have been shipwrecked, a night and a day I have drifted at sea.

26   I have taken a great number of journeys, in which I was exposed to danger from rivers, danger from robbers, danger from my own countrymen, danger from Gentiles, danger in the city, danger in the wilderness, danger at sea, danger from false brothers.

27   I have been involved in labor and hardship, many sleepless nights, hunger and thirst, many occasions when there was no food, cold and nakedness.

28   And besides these outward trials, there is the daily burden of oversight that grows out of my concern for all of the churches.

29   Who is weak, and I am not weak? Who stumbles, and I am not upset?

30   If I have to boast, I shall boast about the things that show my weakness.

---

ber, I'm speaking foolishly in doing so). And then...comes that great list of labors and hardships that Paul presents (vv. 22-29). If you thought the list in Chapter 6 was unbeatable, then read this one again; it tops it! I won't take these items on one by one, but will simply remind you of the great value of comparing Paul's sufferings with those of your counselees when they claim their sufferings are the worst ever borne by a human being (as many seem to think).

In verses 28 and 29 Paul reveals something of his intense involvement with the churches. Though he didn't let it hinder him, he *did* "carry home" problems that he faced daily in his task of apostolic oversight. There was no stoic indifference in Paul. Far from it. Read verse 29. Freudian "professional distance," fortunately, was unknown to him. I say "fortunately" because otherwise we would never have had the Corinthian letters.

But I boast about the things that show my weakness, if you will notice (v. 30). I didn't do anything; it was God who achieved it all. I was even lowered over the wall of Damascus in a stinking fish basket! That shows you how lowly I became in the service of Christ. In the next chapter Paul will continue his foolish boasting, taking still another tack.

But for now, notice one more fact. Paul has spent the lion's share of this epistle defending his apostleship. The reason, of course, was because with it stood or fell the message he preached and the honor of the Christ

31 The God and Father of the Lord Jesus, Who is blessed forever, knows that I am not lying.

32 In Damascus the ethnarch of King Aretas guarded the city of Damascus in order to seize me,

33 but I was lowered through an opening in the wall in a rope basket and escaped out of his hands.

---

he represented. It was not the strategy of the troublemakers at Corinth to challenge Paul's message directly; they knew better than to try that. Instead, they tried to undermine the man, thereby invalidating all he taught. The tactic is still used today. Notice that the arguments of those who oppose biblical counseling center on emotional issues. Those who oppose will not engage the battle in terms of the issues at stake, the truth or error of what is said. Innuendoes are voiced. People are attacked in their persons. The system is caricatured. Whenever you see this—beware.

Consequently it is necessary for you, as a biblical counselor, to defend your integrity even when (like Paul) you feel like a fool doing so. Remember, it is not yourself you are defending; it is God's truth. And never hesitate to call deceit "deceit."

CHAPTER 12

1 I have to boast, although there is no advantage in doing so; I shall come next to visions and revelations from the Lord.

2 I know a person in Christ, who fourteen years ago was snatched away to the third heaven (whether in his body or outside of his body I don't know, but God does).

3 I know this person—whether in his body or outside of his body I don't know (God knows)—

4 was snatched away to Paradise and heard ineffable words that it is not permissible for a human to speak.

5 I shall boast about a person like that, but I won't boast about myself, except about my weaknesses.

Paul continues his defense. He now boasts (foolishly, as he said) about visions and revelations. Should anyone doubt whether Paul thought that he was bringing new revelation to the churches, let him read this chapter again. It should set those doubts to rest. The Lord Jesus had appeared to him on the Damascus road; He stood by him at other crucial times. Paul was a man often in direct contact with Jesus, receiving and imparting revelation (v. 1). Because he is embarrassed to do so, he eliminates the usual first person from verses 2-5. Instead, he stands off and regards himself from the outside as one who was unusual because he was a recipient of revelation. It is not he himself, in and of himself, that he is discussing, but himself only as an instrument the Lord used to impart truth to His church. That he was really speaking of himself as the one caught up into the third heaven[1] (Paradise) is clear because a) he is boasting about himself over against the troublemakers (v. 1), and b) in verse 7 he slips back into the first person singular saying that he was given a thorn in the flesh so that he wouldn't become conceited about the tremendous revelations that he received.

When caught up to heaven, Paul says, the experience was so all-engrossing he doesn't know whether he went in his body or out of it.

---

1. The first "heaven" is the atmosphere (where the "birds of heaven" fly). The second heaven is where the "host of heaven" (sun, moon and starts) are. The third heaven is where God is.

6   If I did want to boast, however, I wouldn't be a fool, since I would be speaking the truth. But I will stop with this so that nobody will gain a higher opinion of me than what he sees me do or hears about me.

7   So that I wouldn't become conceited about these tremendous revelations, I was given a thorn in the flesh, a messenger of Satan to slap me around, so that I wouldn't become conceited.

8   Three times I pleaded with the Lord about this problem, that He would take it away from me;

9   but He said to me: "My help is sufficient for you; My power is fully evident in weakness." So then, I am all the more happy to boast about my weaknesses, that Christ's power might overshadow me.

Interesting that Paul had no difficulty postulating the possibility of an OBE (out-of-body-experience). Because of this passage, in which Paul contemplates the real possibility of such a thing, a Christian counselor must not dismiss out-of-hand reports of OBEs. However insincere most of these may be, however misinterpreted are nearly all the rest, it is *conceivable* (N.B., I did not say more than that) that, rarely, such a thing may occur. If it does, however, it will not be in order to receive revelation from Jesus Christ since that is now complete.

What we wish to focus on is not the heavenly experience—Paul heard ineffable words he couldn't repeat—but on the thorn he was given following the revelations and visions. He must not become conceited over his unusual experience. Nor should others think more highly of him than he does because he went to the third heaven and returned (v. 6).

God gave Paul a thorn in the flesh: a physical infirmity. There is a good possibility that it had to do with his eyesight. The principle is this: privilege may lead to pride. As a result, God may render one weak in some other respect to keep his head from swelling. Satan was the instrument that God used to bring about the affliction to Paul's body. In contrast to what is normal for a Christian (cf. I John 5:18, 19), Satan was allowed to touch Paul's body. This, as in that other instance revealed in Job 1-2, seems exceptional. The case is not the norm in either place since the situations that brought on the afflictions also were out of the norm.

But the basic principle remains. God may bring some humbling affliction (or other experience) to those to whom He has given rare privileges in order to keep them from conceit. Paul prayed three times for this affliction to pass, but the Lord spoke directly to him and said "No." Rather, He replied, I will give you grace to bear up under it and, thereby,

10 That is why I am content with weaknesses, with insults, with needs, with persecutions and difficulties for Christ's sake; whenever I am weak, then I am powerful!

11 I have become a fool, but you made me do it, since I should have been commended by you. I am in no way inferior to these super-apostles, even though I am nothing.

12 The signs of the true apostles were performed among you with great patience, by signs and by wonders and by supernatural works.

---

you will be a living demonstration of the fact that anything you accomplish is the result of My power, not your own (vv. 8, 9).

Because his weakness and affliction were a means of glorifying the Lord Jesus, Paul was elated—even about this (v. 9)! Counselees may learn much from verse 9. Moreover, the weaker he became the more powerful he was because the power was Christ's (v. 10). Let the insults, persecutions and difficulties come; they are only occasions for Christ to manifest His power through me (v. 10).

Not all prayer is answered in the negative; nor should one stop praying after three times. The Lord cut off additional prayer in Paul's case because He wanted him to know that there was a good reason for the thorn to remain. Since such direct revelation does not come our way today there is no reason to cease praying for matters. Indeed, again and again, we are exhorted to "pray without ceasing," which does not mean pray all day long, but does mean don't give up on prayer. Persist like the woman who came again and again to the unjust judge.

Paul has played the fool by offering these various proofs of his apostleship. But he will still mention one more (vv. 11, 12): **the signs of a true apostle**. This is an interesting point. Signs were given in order to help people identify a true apostle. They were, as he says, miraculous works and gifts of the Spirit (v. 12). Those who think that any and every Christian may receive such signs directly from Christ *are mistaken. If this were true, then they would no longer be signs of a true apostle.* If I told you that our church was meeting in a house on such and such a street, but that you'd have no trouble identifying it because it had a sign out front reading "Associate Reformed Presbyterian Church," you'd be reassured that there would be no trouble identifying the new church. But if, when you arrived, you saw nothing but identical houses, each with the same sign reading "ARPC," the sign of our church would no longer be a sign of it at all. It would be worthless so far as its sign-value is concerned. If every Christian had immediate access to the same signs and wonders, as some suppose,

13   How were you inferior to the rest of the churches, except that I didn't make myself a burden to you? Forgive me for this wrong!

14   Here I am ready to come to you for the third time, and I won't burden you now, because I'm not after what you have; I want you. Children ought not to lay up funds for their parents, but parents for their children.

---

they would lose their sign value. They were signs of a true apostle, says Paul.

How then did others receive these signs? We know from I Corinthians that they did. After the Jewish and Gentile Pentecosts (Acts 2, 10) on which occasions signs came directly to mark these unique, once-for-all events, signs were given by the laying on of the apostles' hands (cf. the gifts imparted to the Samaritans and to the Ephesians). Moreover, in Acts 14:3 miracles and gifts of the Spirit are said to have accredited the Lord Jesus Christ as God's Messiah. And in Hebrews 2:3-4 God is said to testify to the truth of His new revelation by them. Signs and wonders were given to the Apostles in order to mark them out as apostles. When they imparted these gifts to others, it was clear to everyone that they were mediated through apostolic persons (cf. Romans 1:12). That, of course, is Paul's argument here: you can know that I am a true apostle by the miracles that I have done. And Corinth was not inferior in the reception of gifts from Paul (v. 13); he had freely given them all to the church (cf. I Corinthians 1:7).

People are confused about the gifts of the Spirit. Sometimes this confusion leads to counseling issues. See my discussion in chapters 12 and 14 of I Corinthians for more details. There is also material in the commentary on Ephesians 2:20 concerning the temporary rather than permanent offices in the church. Keep people oriented to the fact that the signs and miracles were given to authenticate temporary, revelatory officers and the messages they delivered to the church, and you will help them to stay on track.

Paul says, I'm about to come to you. I don't want what you have, I want *you*! I am like a parent. I don't expect anything from you; I should be giving to you as any good parent would. Here is an important principle, given incidentally but unmistakably. While children are obligated to care for aged parents, earlier on parents should not expect the children to give to them. It ought to be the other way around. When working with selfish parents who want everything from their grown children but will never

15 So I most gladly will spend and be spent for the sake of your souls. Am I loved all the less because I love you all the more?

16 Let that be—I didn't burden you; but being crafty did I catch you by tricks?

17 I took advantage of you through somebody I sent you, didn't I?

18 I pleaded with Titus to go and sent the brother along with him; it was Titus who took advantage of you, wasn't it? Didn't we walk by the same Spirit? Didn't we take the same steps?

19 Have you been thinking all along that we were defending ourselves to you? You're wrong. It is before God that we have been speaking for Christ; and everything has been done to build you up.

---

give them anything to help them along in those crucial, early days of marriage, you will be able to help by the careful application of this verse to the situation. This does not imply indulgence, but it does indicate help (v. 14).

So, like a good parent, he will spend and be spent on them. So do you love me less because I love you more? Often that is the way with ungrateful children, to whom this passage also may be referred. There is often a bad attitude of expectation on the part of ungrateful children. "Isn't that what I deserve? After all, I'm their child, aren't I?" No gratitude (see II Timothy 3). Those on both sides of the relationship should learn from verses 14 and 15.

Here is one more indication of how we lived among you, says Paul— I didn't burden you or catch you through some crafty means. I suppose (sarcasm again) I tricked you by sending Titus to take advantage of you. Was that what happened? Or wasn't he willing to give himself to you rather than get, just as I am (vv. 16-18)? There is no need to expatiate on the matter of the use of sarcasm; elsewhere I have said something about it. But for now, just this: sarcasm is a powerful tool. It may be used fruitfully in counseling, *only if used wisely*. What makes the difference? If along with the sarcasm there is a clear indication of the loving concern of the counselor and His Lord, you can get away with it. Otherwise it will drive people away. Sarcasm is used by Paul to bring conviction of sin.

Well, Paul is about to conclude his long defense. So he sums up with an important word: Please don't think we have been defending *ourselves* throughout all of this. No, heaven forbid! Who am I? No one. No, it is for Christ's sake that we have gone into this elaborate defense of our apostleship. And all I have said—even the most recent sarcasm—has been to

20 I'm afraid that when I come I may not find you as I want to find you, and that you may find me to be what you don't want to find; That there may be strife, jealousy, anger, selfishness, slander, gossip, conceit, disturbances.

21 I'm afraid that when I come again my God may humble me before you, and I shall mourn over many of those who have sinned before and haven't repented of the uncleanness and sexual sin and sensualness that they have practiced.

---

build you up (v. 19). I have written because I want to find you free from the things I fear may be there (strife, jealousy, anger, selfishness, slander, gossip, conceit, disturbances). If I do you won't want to find me the way you will either (v. 20)! I don't want to be humbled by finding it necessary to mourn over the many who have sinned and never repented of their uncleanness, sexual sin and sensualness. Please don't let me come and find a situation like that!

Paul's was a real ministry of counseling. He dealt with the real problems you must face, counselor. He knew the bitterness of the sins listed in the last two verses of this chapter, how they ruined lives and churches. But—and don't miss this—he didn't give up on people struggling with these sins. He talked to them about them and faithfully ministered to them. He insisted on repentance on their part and cleaning up their act. Paul had a true pastor's heart. Do you?

CHAPTER 13

1 This is the third time that I am coming to you. Every charge
must be substantiated by the mouth of two or three witnesses.

2 I said it before to those who sinned before while I was present with
you the second time, and now I say it in advance, while I am absent, to the
rest of you, that when I come to you again I won't spare them,

3 since you are seeking a proof that Christ is speaking in me. He is not
weak toward you, but is powerful among you.

4 It is true that He was crucified in weakness, but He lives by God's
power. And it is true that we are weak in Him, but we shall live with Him
by God's power for you.

5 Test yourselves to see whether you are in the faith; approve yourselves. Don't you realize that Jesus Christ is in you, unless, of course, you
turn out to be counterfeits?

6 I hope that you will know that we aren't counterfeits.

Paul is preparing for the worst. He has listed all sorts of things he is
afraid he may encounter when he comes to Corinth for the third time. So
he lays down God's ground rule: **Every charge must be substantiated
by the mouth of two or three witnesses**. That was His rule in the Old
Testament, and it is still His rule in the church of the New Testament.
How important it is for you as a counselor to insist on this rule! If counselees are known for anything, it is for their accusations (many of which
are false) against one another. A careful application of this rule, in which
you refuse to hear charges made without adequate evidence presented by
reliable witnesses, will cut down on most of this.

I am saying it once and for all—those who have sinned by attacking
my authority as an apostle will not be spared when I come (v. 2). You
want proof? Well, that will be it. You will see for yourselves the power of
God displayed in your midst (vv. 3, 4). Christ is the One who is in question, not me; and you are about to see His power among you. True, He
was weak in the crucifixion, but He lives by the power of God. We are
weak also, but there is nothing but power as He works through us (v. 4).

Some of you may not be saved; there is good reason, as I have indicated, for saying this. Therefore I urge you, test yourselves to be sure you
are saved. Jesus Christ is in you or you are counterfeits (v. 5). And after
all, as I have said, I hope you now realize that we are not counterfeits (v.

7   Now we pray to God that you won't do wrong, not that we may appear approved, but that you may do good, even if we may seem to be counterfeits.

8   We can't do anything against the truth, but only for the truth.

9   We are glad when we are weak and you are strong; and what we pray for is that you may be fully restored.

10   It is for this reason that I'm writing these things while I'm absent, so that when I'm present I won't have to cut off any of you by the authority that the Lord gave me for building up and not for tearing down.

11   Finally, brothers, good-bye. Mend your ways, pay attention to my appeal, agree with one another, be at peace, and the God of love and peace will be with you.

12   Greet one another with a holy kiss.

13   All the saints greet you.

14   May help from the Lord Jesus Christ, and love from God and fellowship from the Holy Spirit be with all of you.

---

6). And as far as that goes, it really doesn't matter if you think we are counterfeits so long as you do the right thing (v. 7). There isn't anything that can be done against truth. Only for it (v. 8). God's truth will prevail. If our being weak means that you are strong, that is what counts (v. 9). We pray that you will be fully restored.

I could come and deal sharply with you. I don't want to do that. That's why I'm writing now. Please get all these matters straightened up before I come. I want to use my authority for building up rather than tearing down (v. 10).

Then his last words: Listen to what I've written; mend your ways, get along with one another. May God bless you.

It was a powerful letter, among Paul's writings unique for its personal appeal. If Paul is telling you anything in it as a counselor, it is that you must love your counselees dearly, give yourself to them, be willing to take it on the chin for their sake, put Christ forward first, and forget yourself. There are noble ideals set forth in it that are unattainable in the absolute but more and more attainable, in part, as one works at them in the power and wisdom of the Spirit. Don't miss what God can do for you *as a person* through His wisdom exhibited in II Corinthians!